Minimalist Budget:

How to Use Smart Money System and Live Minimalist Lifestyle. How to Turn Bad Credit into Good Credit

Contents

Introduction

Study shows that the typical American has a credit score of 680 based on the VantageScore protocol and 703 when using the FICO score model as its base. Now, if you have checked your score recently and found that you are above the national average, then you are on the right path. According to studies, around 21 percent of Americans today fall below that average when it comes to credit scores.

Here's the thing though – what exactly can a good credit score for you? And if you fall below the average – what can you do to improve it?

This book is all about helping you improve your financial standing by addressing your credit score and turning it around from bad to good or, if you already have a good score, then from good to better. We take this financial responsibility one step further by teaching you the key techniques on how to make sure that your credit score retains that excellent number even as you manage to perfectly juggle your finances.

Now – most people will tell you that the best way to live your life money-wise is to not have any form of debt at all. Don't borrow money so that you don't have to worry about paying back money and interest. Some people would go so far as to say that you should only live through a cash-basis system. Unfortunately, as good as it may sound, this approach is far from realistic.

You need to borrow money. You also need to pay it back.

A credit score puts you in the map. It's indicative of who you are as a borrower and while this might not serve you NOW, it will definitely serve you in the future when you do need to borrow something.

Not having any type of credit on the other hand removes you completely from the map. It makes you invisible.

Reading this book is the first step of your journey towards financial responsibility by placing yourself on the good side of the social economy. By the end of this book, you should be able to accomplish several things:

- Understand the value of a good credit score
- Know the factors that make up a good credit score
- Find out how to improve your credit score
- Learn how to dispute errors you find in your credit score
- Change your spending habits to sustain a good credit score

By the end of this book, there is every hope that you'll be able to improve your financial standing – not just in your own eyes but also in the eyes of the people who extend you credit.

Chapter 1: Your Financial Situation – Explaining Credit Scores

Since you are reading this book, I trust that you already have about what score you hold. Most people don't even bother knowing their credit score until they feel like they're ready to make a major purchase – like buying a house or a car on loan. For some people, by the time they address their credit score, it's already too late.

What Is It Exactly?

Well, keep this brief. In simplest terms, your credit score is a scoring system used by financial companies to judge whether you are a good borrower. If you have a bad credit score, a lender can choose not to extend you a loan or if they do extend a loan, they're going to place a high interest rate on it to counterbalance the chances of you not paying. A good credit score means you are more likely to pay your loans, which means that lenders aren't as cautious and will gladly extend you the loan with just a small interest rate.

Who Computes Credit Scores

Credit score are computed by the credit bureaus who issue these scores in the first place. The top 3 major bureaus are TransUnion, Equifax, and Experian.

Does this mean that all three follow the same formula for computation? Not really. In fact, there are TWO providers of formula for computing credit score. The most popular one is the one developed by Fair Isaac Corporation or FICO. Lately however, the VantageScore system is gaining popularity and is also being used to determine your financial standing.

Confused yet? You shouldn't be. Let's discuss this as simply as possible. The 3 Credit Bureaus collect your data and use either the FICO system or the VantageScore system to compute your credit score. What's the difference between these two formulas however and how exactly would they affect you?

The Tri-Bureau System of Vantage Score

One of the distinguishing factors between FICO and Vantage is the method of scoring in relation to the credit bureau. VantageScore likes to keep things simple by providing a computation that's similar across the board. Hence, the computation of your score for Experian is the same as with TransUnion and Equifax.

FICO's Bureau Specific Model
On the other hand, FICO likes to keep their computations bureau specific. Hence, the formula used for Equifax may be different from that of TransUnion, and Experian. This is why you would get different scores from each Bureau. There is also the fact that each Bureau may use entirely different data for computation. For example, some lenders may send only to Equifax while others may send their data exclusively with TransUnion. These differences can lead to a variance between the scores you get throughout the year.

How Credit Scores are Computed
The good news is that the formula for computing your credit score isn't exactly a State secret. There is a scoring system that's developed by Fair Isaac and used by the three major credit bureaus to

arrive at an exact number. This formula takes five (5) factors into consideration.

There is your payment history which takes up 35% of the score. Your existing debt which is around 30% of the computation. The length of your credit history takes up 15% and the type of credit takes up 10% of the score. Finally, there is new credit inquires with 10%, totaling to 100% of your score.

Now, does this mean that you can do your own computation? Well, not really. You can attempt to do an estimate, but the official numbers come from the credit bureaus. These are the numbers utilized by the banks and other money lenders to judge whether you are worthy of an extended loan or not. Therefore, it's no use trying to question the computation itself since the formula varies. The only factor you can question would be the numbers used in the formula.

Your ability to compute your own credit score is also hampered by the fact that you might not have all the information you need to make this happen. Computation covers your financial transactions over a period of years – thus the difficulty.

Does this mean there is nothing you can do about your credit score? Of course not. There are ways you can dispute erroneous entries in your history, or have certain entries stricken out. It's not advisable to completely put your trust on credit bureaus when it comes to record keeping. Later on, in this book, well talk about how to have your credit history corrected in order to reflect your true (and hopefully better!) credit score.

What's a Good Score? Interpreting your Score

Credit scores are ranked from 300 to 850 with a higher score equivalent to a better standing in the eyes of lenders. Depending on your placement on the scale, you can fall under any of the following categories: Excellent, Very Good, Good, Fair, and Poor.

If you already know your credit score, here's where you fall in the range:

- Excellent or Exceptional: 800 to 850
- Very Good: 740 to 799

- Good: 670 to 739
- Fair: 580 to 669
- Poor: 300 to 579

Understand that because there are two credit score computations, there are also two "average" credit scores depending on whether its FICO or Vantage. Both however use the same scale of 300 to 850.

What Debts are Included in Credit Scores?

There are tons of misconception about credit scores and what financial transactions are included in them. Later on, we'll talk more about the myths and facts surrounding your credit history, but for now – let's focus a bit on what actually forms part of your credit score.

- Credit card debt
- Secured loans
- Unsecured loans
- Unpaid and overdue debts
- Late debt payments

Now, this might seem like a vague list, but you want to keep in mind that when it comes to credit scores, the exclusions are more easily defined than the inclusions. That is, there is a definitive list of what is NOT considered when computing your credit score. If you currently owe money that is NOT included in this list, then chances are it forms part of your credit report and thus, affects your overall score.

Here's the list:

- Bank overdrafts
- Child support payments and alimony
- Insurance payments
- Rental payments
- Phone bills and utility bills
- Judgment debts

Credit Score versus Credit History
You might note that we're using both term throughout this book. Keep in mind that there is a big difference between these two terms. Your credit score is basically, well, your score. It identifies where you fall in the spectrum of 300 to 850. Are you in the Very Good, Good, or Exceptional Category?

Your credit history is also known as your credit report. These two terms are interchangeable and basically refers to all the transactions that occurred and were factored into computing your credit score. Think of your score as your final grade in a college subject and the report would be all the quizzes, recitations, group projects, and exams you had along the way.

Why Do You Need to Check Your Credit Score?

Now, there are several reasons why you would want to check your credit score on a routine basis. The obvious one here is to prevent identity theft. A complete credit report will show you exactly what financial transactions have been done in your name – and therefore give you the chance to dispute them or rectify the problem quickly. As you can probably tell, identity theft that's been left unrecognized for long periods of time can completely ruin you financially.

Constantly checking your credit score will also give you a chance to correct errors that may be reflected on your account. Credit bureaus are not infallible – there are instances when they make erroneous entries or have outdated information which can drag down your

report. Keeping your history up to date
ensures the accuracy of the information
reflected there.

Chapter 2: The Law on Credit Scores

Before we discuss further about how you can improve your credit score, it's important to first understand the underlying rules and regulations when it comes to credit scores. It's a heavily regulated field and if you want to properly navigate your way through it, you will want to know what laws are concerned, your rights, responsibilities, and obligations under it.

Governing Federal Law – Fair Credit Reporting Act

Abbreviated as the FCRA, this is the primary law that governs credit reporting. The goal is to make sure that consumer reporting agencies provide only fair and accurate information while keeping the privacy of their files. It covers not just the major credit bureaus but also specialty agencies.

Right to Information of What's in Your File

This is perhaps the most important one. As a consumer, you are entitled to one free credit history disclosure every year or for every 12 months. This is not automatic – you'll have to put in a request and the credit bureau is under the obligation to comply with that request. The good thing here is that each credit bureau is under this obligation. Hence, every 12 months – you can get a free credit report from Equifax, TransUnion, and Experian without expenses on your part.

Note that there is only one website that processes annual credit reports for free. That's the AnnualCreditReport.com domain. Any other domain that claims to offer free credit reports – aside from the official website of the credit bureau - are unauthorized.

In addition to those mandated instances of free disclosure, special circumstances will also let you request a free report outside of the once a year situation. This can happen if any of the circumstances are present:

- If there is an adverse action against you using your credit score
- You are a victim of identity theft or there has been a fraud alert on your file

- Inaccurate information is present in your file because of fraud
- You are currently unemployed but will be looking for employment in the next 60 days
- You are on public assistance

Note that when requesting your credit report, you'll be asked to provide proper identification. This can mean sending them even your social security number. This being the case, it's crucial to request only from proper and accredited bureaus, otherwise you might encounter problems on privacy.

UPDATE: As of the year 2020, every US citizen can now get an additional 6 free credit reports every year. That's on top of the one credit report you get every year from Equifax. Note that this is only available through Equifax and not anywhere else. Hence, you get a total of 7 free credit reports from Equifax and then a free one from the other two credit bureaus. Note though that 6 free credit reports are only available until the year 2026.

Right to Information of Adverse Use of your File

Let's say you wanted to rent a particular property. Unfortunately, the landlord rejected your application after accessing your credit report. Upon rejection, the landlord is compelled to inform you about the source of that information which includes the name, phone number, and address of the agency.

Right to Dispute
If you think your credit score is inaccurate, you are also in the position to dispute these problem areas. Perhaps there is a debt there that's long been paid but still remains on your history? Perhaps there are outdated information there or debts that are 10 years old? If that's the case, then you can ask the credit bureau to update their records in order to reflect the true status of your finances. You can have these stricken out of the record and there is a precise process for that. Later on, we'll talk about how to improve your credit score by launching disputes.

Right to Privacy
Your credit report is private and may only be divulged to people who have a legitimate reason to request it. The law provides for a list of people who have a

valid need for a credit report – such as your insurer, landlord, employer, creditor, or other businesses that are transacting with you on the basis of credit. Note that consent is needed on your part in order to make this possible. Hence, before any access is made, you will be asked to make a written expression of consent to have your files sent to a third party.

Right to Remedies on Problematic Credit Scores
Identity theft is a very real thing nowadays and if someone manages to get a hold of your identity, they may mess up your finances. This is where Security Freeze and Fraud Alert comes in. These are remedies you can use to prevent or alert you to any fraud.

A Security Freeze works by preventing agencies from releasing your credit report without first getting your consent. This way, you will be instantly alerted if someone is trying to open a credit card or get a loan using your name.

A Fraud Alert on the other hand is a warning to creditors to first verify information before extending any sort of credit to someone. It spans 1 year and must be renewed each time if you want to always be alerted if someone is trying to open an account using your name. If you've been the victim of identity theft, you can also get what is known as an Extended Fraud Alert which lasts up to 7 years.

The Fair Debt Collection Practices Act (FDCPA)

This particular law was enacted as far back as 1977. It was made to make sure that debt collectors do not abuse their rights when trying to collect debts from borrowers. Note however that this law regulates third party collectors and not primary lenders. For example, if your credit card company sold the debt to a third party, this third party will be the one regulated by the FDCPA.

So, what exactly is provided by the FDCPA? Here's what you should know:

• Debt collectors can only call you from 8 am to 9pm. This period should be based on your local time zone regardless of where the collection agency is located.

- Debt collectors are required to keep your debt information private. Hence, they cannot talk to anyone else about any unpaid debts you may have under their account. The only exception here would be your spouse and your lawyer. However, if the debt collector will contact a third party in order to gain access to your information, then this would be an allowed deviation.

- Debt collectors are not allowed to call you at work if you have previously told them that this is prohibited.

- If the debt collector constantly contacts you, you have the right to send them a certified mail asking the collecting company to stop contacting you. A certified mail is the best option in this situation to help you keep track of any communication. Note that this can backfire because the collecting agency may choose to file a lawsuit against you if you continue to evade the debt.

- A debt collector is required to send you written communication detailing how much you owe, what company you owe it to, and instructions on what you should do to pay the debt or dispute it if it does not belong to you or it has already been paid.

- Finally, debt collectors are not allowed to threaten, harass, curse or seize money from your bank account without previous approval. They also cannot tell you that you will be arrested if you fail to make payments.
- Currently, it's not possible for a person to be jailed in the United States for non-payment of a civil debt.

What does this have to do with your credit score? Collection agencies indicate that your debt is well past due and has led to negative markings on your credit report. This does not mean that you don't have to pay the account anymore. However, for purposes of improving your credit score, delinquent debts must be considered low priority. This being the case, knowing your rights will help you resist the pressure of paying off these delinquent debts until and unless you have paid the most recent ones.

CARES Act

Also known as the Coronavirus Aid Relief and Economic Security Act (CARES), this particular legislation was passed in response to the financial crisis triggered by Covid-19 Pandemic. With the lockdown that came with the pandemic, many businesses have been forced to close, impacting the employment status of many Americans. As of August 2020, unemployment rate rose in the United States by as much as 1.4 million.

The CARES Act works by changing the way credit is reported during Coronavirus pandemic. For example, you were supposed to make payments in July 2020 but failed to do so because of the outbreak. Upon agreement with your creditor this failure to pay shall not be reported as delinquent. Instead, it will be reported as current thereby ensuring that you will not have late payments on your record. Simply put, the CARES Act imposed a temporary suspension of the running time

The complexity happens when you were already delinquent at the time of the Coronavirus pandemic. For example, you were supposed to pay off the loan by August 2019. Upon agreement with your creditor the status of your account will be reported as delinquent until you manage to bring it back to current. Once this happens, the creditor will change the status of your account to current.

Note however, that the CARES Act was drafted in response to the unique situation of 2020. Therefore, it only applies to situations occurring between January 31, 2020 and July 25, 2020. As of this writing, the pandemic is still active in the United States, the CARES Act will continue to operate until 120 days after the pandemic is declared over by the Federal Government.

But what exactly does agreement mean within the scope of the CARES Act? This simply means that an agreement between you and the creditor must be made with respect to partial payments or to modify the loan or to put the loan in forbearance or any other agreement that offers relief

Chapter 3: General Information on Credit Scores

As mentioned, there are three major credit bureaus that keep your credit history and formulate a credit score for the use of those who are entering in a financial transaction with you.

The Credit Bureaus – How they Work

All three credit bureaus work the same way – they collect credit-related information about you, compile them, and calculate a score which they then provide to third parties who pay for them. Don't worry though – this is not a violation of your privacy because the third parties are often those who have been given special access by the law. This includes creditors, landlords, insurers, banks, and other lending institutions.

The way these credit reporting companies use the information they get from you is heavily regulated by the law, specifically the FCRA or the Fair Credit Reporting Act. We already talked about those rights under a previous Chapter of this book.

Who Runs These Credit Bureaus?

Understand that the credit bureaus are NOT run by the government. The federal government may regulate how they handle the data they receive – but their day to day operations are not controlled by the national or even the state government. These credit bureaus are run like businesses and they make their money by providing banks and lending institutions with credit scores to aid them in their financial transactions.

Discrepancies of the Three Scores

There are a few differences in how computation is done, which naturally leads to discrepancies of the three scores. We already talked about the fact that there is FICO and there is VantageScore protocols used to compute the score. There is also the fact that each credit bureau might be operating on different sets of data. While all three will receive the similar information, it could be interpreted through different ways and therefore presented in varying ways. Some bureaus may provide a more updated setup while others may be a few transactions behind.

This is why it's important to do your own check to guarantee that updates are reflected on your credit history.

Chapter 4: What Affects Your Credit Scores

A lot of things are considered when computing your credit score – which is why it's not possible for you to compute it yourself. Even if you have the formula, all the information necessary to do the computation might not be available to you.

Factors Considered in Your Credit Score and What it Means

We already talked about the main components of the formula leading to your credit score. In this part of the book, we'll try to explore those factors further and see exactly how they impact your numbers.

Payment History

This will cover all payments you've made on your credit card, installment loans, mortgages, retail accounts, and your open accounts in finance companies. Included are also any record of bankruptcies, judgments, liens, suits, or foreclosures under your name. The history takes into account not just how much debt you owe but also how much you should be paying each month and whether you are meeting those payments.

Length of Credit History
Credit scores are no reliant on all you credit transactions from the time you started borrowing money. Typically, the history only goes as far back as seven years or ten years. Hence, anything beyond that time period will no longer be taken into account when computing your score. Lenders will take into account the fact of proper credit management during such time. Did you pay your debts? Do you often take out multiple loans? Do you wait to pay off your existing loans before starting a new one?

Credit Utilization
This is just another term of the actual amount you currently owe. It answers the question – how deeply in debt are you? Obviously, if you have excessive debts, then any additional financial burden may make it harder for you to pay off existing obligations. But how much is just the right amount to make you look good in this aspect of the check? Well, the rule of thumb is that any credit you have must not be more than 30 percent of the credit limit in your card. Hence, let's say you

have a $10,000 credit card limit on your account. The debt in there must not be more than $3,000, otherwise, you already have negative credit utilization.

Now, in the course of this discussion, you'll also read about Credit Utilization Ratio which answers the question: Out of the amount you are allowed to borrow, how much have you actually borrowed? We'll talk more about that in the Chapter specifically for credit cards since this is where it usually happens. Right now, what you should know is that the credit utilization ratio should follow the 30 percent pattern as well in order for you to maintain a good standing in your credit score.

Types of Credit You Have
This talks about your credit mix which is basically the different types of accounts you currently have. This often includes credit cards, loans on installment, mortgage loans, retail accounts, and so on. The main factor determined here is if you are using these accounts in the way they're meant to be used. For example, let's say you just purchased a car using your credit card. That's hardly a good way to utilize your existing credit

considering the high interest rate often associated with credit card purchases. If this happens, then this can negatively affect your credit score.

Revolving Debt and Installment Debt
It's also important to make the distinction between a revolving debt and an installment debt. A revolving debt refers primarily to your credit card provider. This has a revoiving balance, or you basically get a new payable amount each month. There is a predetermined limit and any purchases you make is added on to your existing debt – to be paid at a fixed time each month. Since it's revolving, the debt is subject to change – which means that it can go from 300USD to 600USD to 200USD in span of three months, depending on your spending and payment habits.

The other type is the installment debt which primarily refers to your mortgage loans, auto loans, student loans, and other big debts. There is no revolving amount – the monthly payments do not change and aside from the interest rate, there is really no change to speak of.

Both debts require on time payments so that failure in one will lead to a negative mark on your card. However, understand that of the two – the revolving debt often has a higher mark on your credit report. This is because the credit card debt is the one that's factored into debt to credit ratio. This is the one with the ceiling and the revolving debt is compared to the ceiling. In contrast, the total amount of your loan in student debts or mortgage is NOT heavily factored as a ceiling.

New Credit
This refers to any new credit you might be thinking of getting. Hence, if you've made inquiries about opening new credit cards or taking out a loan, this information will be added in computing the credit score. This falls into the debt to credit ratio which tells a lender whether you are still borrowing within the amount you are actually allowed to have.

Hard and Soft Inquiries
Also called as "hard or soft pull", these are transactions that may or may not affect your credit score. A soft pull would be any transaction you enter into relating to credit scores that don't have any effect on it. A good example would be ordering

your credit score or when the credit card company offers you a new line based on your history. Since they're the ones who offered you a plan, this doesn't affect negatively on your credit score.

On the other hand, there are the hard pulls or hard inquiries that will do something to your credit score. This often occurs when a bank or credit card company requests your information due to an inquiry. Hence, each time you inquire into a bank or credit card company in order to open a new account – this count as a hard pull on your score. This is especially true if you are already near your maximum ceiling for credit or if the hard pulls happen quickly over a short period of time.

But what if you are simply shopping through different lenders in order to find the cheapest one? The good news is that this is something the bureau has taken into account. In fact, FICO even has a term for it – rate shopping. Hence, if you make hard inquiries continuously within a 45-day period, this will all be counted as just one.

Chapter 5: Credit Score Impact on Financial Security

Everyone knows that they're supposed to have a "good" credit score – but few actually really how this translates to the real world.

One thing you have to remember is that a bad credit score has a rippling effect on anything and everything you choose to do in life. It can make things harder for you as it triggers an accumulative disadvantage. That is, once your credit score hits numbers considered to be "bad", it collapses onto itself so that your lifestyle can actually become more expensive to maintain.

What exactly do we mean by that? Here arc somc notable examples you can try to keep in mind:

Let's Illustrate This First on Major Loans

Let's say you've decided to borrow $300,000. It's payable for the next 30 years and it comes with a fixed rate. Now, if were 'going to just look at the principal itself, the $300,00 loan payable over a period of 30 years will require that you pay a minimum of $833.33 per month.

That's just the principal of course. The fixed rate will be determined by the credit score you have. A "good" credit score can net you an interest rate of around 3 percent. Doing the math, this means that on top of the $833.33 per month payments, you'll have to pay an interest of $25 per month so you'll be remitting $858.33 every month for the next 33 years to pay off the loan.

Now, let's say you have a bad credit score. This could easily mean your interest will take a hike of around 1.5 percent, which means that you'll be paying a 4.5 percent interest rate on your loan just because you have a bad credit score. Doing the math again, that means that on top of the $833.33 per month, you'll be paying $37.5 as an interest rate. Hence, you'll be remitting $870.83 every month for the next 30 years.

That's a $12.5 difference!

Now, you might think that's not a big gap, especially since you are submitting payments on a monthly basis. What's 13 dollars? Here's the catch though – if you look at it as a whole, you might be surprised at how much this amount actually adds up.

With a good credit score, you'll be paying a total of $9000 of pure interest. With a bad one? You'll be paying $13500! That's a $4,500 difference! Think what you could have done with that $4,500 instead!

This is where the impact of a bad credit score really hits you in the face, and this is why I want you to take this book *really* seriously.

But that's just on major loans. You'll find that even without a loan, your credit score can actually impact every aspect of your life..

It Can Raise Daily Expenses

Banks aren't the only ones who make use of your credit score to judge whether you are a good financial risk. There is the credit card company, your cellphone providers, your utility companies, your insurer, and even your landlord can all look into your credit score and adjust transactions with you based on that information.

This impact on daily expenditures is most obvious when we're looking at your credit card interest rate. If you buy your groceries on credit and pay only the minimum amount per month, you could be paying for your tub of ice cream at a slightly higher cost than someone with a good credit score. Now, that might seem negligible, but remember the computation we did in the previous discussion. Factoring in the interest rate, you could be paying around $1.5 more for meat and if you buy meat often, that can add up to hundreds if not thousands of dollars in a span of a year.

It Can Affect your Employment Status
You need a job to pay your bills and raise your credit score. Unfortunately, a bad credit score can keep you from being hired. It's a nasty cycle – but it's not an unbreakable one.

Why do employers even bother checking in the first place? A bad credit score is often interpreted as a bay management style of finances. An employee hurting for cash is more likely to steal or embezzle money or merchandise from the business. It's not universally true of course, but statistics show that around 47 percent of employers still follow this hiring approach.

Maybe Affect Your Love Life?

A study shows that credit score has a huge impact on how people will see you as a lifetime partner material. A bad credit score can easily discourage a person from dating you. Of course, one might argue that credit scores aren't exactly the subject of dates – but just keep in mind that it's a topic that will eventually be answered later on.

One interesting study about credit score is that it can predict how your relationship would go or who you end up with. Report from the Board of Governors of Federal Reserve in 2015 shows that people with good credit reports tend to end up together and stay together. This isn't exactly surprising since individuals who are financially responsible are more likely to look for partners who have the same mental state as them. Now, it might be a farfetched claim that a good credit score can help you have a good relationship. However, there is nothing wrong with making the effort, especially if there is a chance that it would improve your chances of finding a long-term partner.

Good Score Offers Side Perks
On the flipside, the beauty of a good credit score goes beyond simply having a lower interest rate. That's a direct and obvious effect of the score – but what about the non-obvious ones?

People with good scores often enjoy side benefits such as being given promotional products, given additional leeway on their accounts, offered bonus points that they can redeem for merchandise, and so on. All of these perks are extended towards good credit score holders in an effort to retain their business and keep them loyal. After all, why would businesses offer this to those with bad credit if there is a good chance that they'll be unpaid?

Chapter 6: Bankruptcy, Marriage, and Guaranties on Credit Score

The relationships you choose to undertake may also have an impact on your credit score such as getting married, becoming divorced, choosing to open a joint account with someone, starting a business, and undertaking to be a surety or a guaranty on a loan in favor of someone. More often than not, people forget about these relationships and are simply shocked when they find their credit score plummeting because of these decisions.

On this Chapter, we'll talk about how these different relationships and transactions will affect your credit score.

On Bankruptcies
Bankruptcy is always a tough time for your finances – but what exactly happens to your credit score if you go through one?

First, let's tackle exactly what bankruptcy does. It's actually a legal proceeding undertaken by people who have more debt than assets. If you think you are overwhelmed by debt and there is no way to recover, you can apply for bankruptcy and have a major portion of your debt wiped out, essentially allowing you to start on a clean slate. Note that we're referring to "majority" of your debt and not all of them because there will be debts that remain. For example, unpaid taxes will still be there, any alimony or child support payments are not wiped out, and if you have unpaid debts arising out of willful and malicious injury to another person – then those will still remain.

Bankruptcy as Part of Your Credit Report

You can be sure that while bankruptcy will wipe out discharged debts, the bankruptcy itself will form part of your credit report. It will stay there for the next 7 or 10 years, depending on the Bankruptcy Chapter you file for. Bankruptcy is in fact, the only matter of public record that shows up in your credit report.

Understand, there are two Bankruptcy Chapters typically applied for by individuals. That's Chapter 7 and Chapter 13.

Chapter 7 is a straight-out bankruptcy declaration. This is when most of your assets are liquidated and used to pay off existing debts for as much as it would stretch out. Remaining debts shall be discharged while some debts will remain because the law doesn't allow them to be discharged – like taxes or child support.

Chapter 13 is not really a bankruptcy but rather, a reorganization of your debt. For example, you currently have 10 different debts with each one carrying a different interest rate. If all these debts prove too much for your finances, a Chapter 13 bankruptcy will consolidate all these debts so that you'll only have to pay one debt under one interest rate. The debt is not discharged – it's organized so that you'll find it easier to handle.

Once you file for bankruptcy, any creditors you may have will stop contacting you to pay for the debt. This is perhaps the most important effect that happens after filing. It affords you the relief of knowing that creditors would stop threatening you over the phone and you now have a straightforward way of handling the financial mess.

How Long with Bankruptcy Last in the Credit Report?

As mentioned, the life of bankruptcy in your credit report can be anywhere from seven to ten years. If you applied for a Chapter 7 Bankruptcy, expect to have it with you for ten years. If you opted for a Chapter 13, it would only start for seven years in your account.

Bankruptcy Lowers Your Credit Score

This is a fairly obvious result of bankruptcy. What's really important is – by how much does your credit score decrease if you file for bankruptcy? More importantly, how will the credit bureaus calculate your score if you declared bankruptcy?

The truth is that there is no exact number of how much your score may plummet. Some people with a good credit score can experience a bigger loss compared to someone who actually had a bad credit score to start with. This is because personal circumstances – as well as the varying information provided by companies – all add up to how the credit score is impacted.

But how exactly is a bankruptcy reflected on your credit report? Well, let's say you have a $10,000 debt on your credit card before filing for bankruptcy. Once the bankruptcy has been allowed, this $10,000 would be discharged. The credit report will still show this $10,000 unpaid debt but with a note that identifies it as "discharged" or "included in bankruptcy". For all intents and purposes, this will be considered as zero balance.

When to declare bankruptcy
Bankruptcy should be a last option for repairing or building your credit score.

It is opted for when no other solution is available. Keep in mind that in most cases, bankruptcy is chosen not as a way to improve your credit score but rather to give you some relief from the creditors compelling you to pay off your debt.

Once you declare bankruptcy you will no longer be pressured into making payments. Keep in mind however, that this record will stay in your credit report for the next ten years. The only upside is that from here on out, you can work towards improving your future financial transactions. It's a form of relief from the pressure and is a good way to handle a situation that leaves you feeling overwhelmed.

So when should you file for bankruptcy? If the following circumstances are present, then declaring bankruptcy is really your best financial decision.

- You already tried negotiating with the credit card companies. Later on, in this book we will talk about debt settlement and debt negotiation which are secondary options for paying off your debt. If you have already done these without promising results, then bankruptcy would be your next course of action. In most cases however, creditors are willing to negotiate with you in terms of payment.
- Assets and income are significantly less than your outstanding debt. Simply put if you theoretically sell your assets and they would still be less than the amount that you owe, then there is no other option but to declare bankruptcy.

Improving your Credit Score after Bankruptcy

The methods for reviving your credit score after bankruptcy versus without it aren't so different. With bankruptcy however, there are just a few extra steps to help make sure that you are taking a better financial path as opposed to your money decisions before.

Oddly enough, people who have a good credit score often suffer more than people who have a bad one upon declaring bankruptcy. For example, a study shows that someone with a score of 680 loses 150 points upon declaring bankruptcy. In contrast, someone with a 780 score loses 240 points upon declaration. When you do the math however, both person plummet to a score of around 530 or 540.

How Marriage Affects your Credit Score

The most important thing you should know here is that even when married – your credit report is your own. It won't merge into one giant super credit report combining your partner's credit and your own. Of course, there are special exceptions here – such as when you have a joint credit account, but we'll talk about that more extensively at a special Chapter of this book.

What about the change in name of the woman after marriage? The switch to the surname of the husband is treated as a mere variation of the person's name. It will be noted on the credit report and financial entries will simply continue as such. A marriage and subsequent divorce will not create a brand new history.

How Guaranties and Sureties Affect your Credit Score

Agreeing to be someone's guarantor or surety will not affect your credit score as long as the principal borrower manages to pay off the debt. What if they failed to do that? Well, now the loan becomes your problem, and this will be reflected in your credit history.

Before we talk more about this, it's important that you first understand what the difference between a guarantor and a surety. As a guarantor, you promise to pay someone else's debt if they fail to pay it on the date required. Hence, the lender must first go to the borrower and if the borrower cannot pay and has zero assets to use for payment, it is only then that the lender can go to you – the guarantor – for payment of the debt. You are second in line when it's time to pay the debt.

Being a surety is another matter entirely. As a surety, you are placed in the same level as the borrower. Hence, if the borrower fails to make payments, the lender can go to you and ask for payment. The main distinction here is that even if the primary borrower still has assets that can be sold to pay for the debt, you cannot raise this as a defense. The lender can go after you regardless of whether the borrower has money or not. Hence, as a surety, your responsibility for the payment of the debt is practically the same as that of the borrower. IIence, if you are going to undertake a transaction, it's often better and safer to be the guarantor instead of being a surety.

In either case, non-payment or even late payments will be reflected on your credit score. In the report, it would be as if you are the person who borrowed the money. Hence, if you want that particular transaction to be removed – you will need to pay for the debt or compel the principal borrower to pay it. Telling the credit bureau that you are merely a guarantor, or a borrower will not absolve you from this negative mark on your account.

The good news is that the story is a bit different if you choose to be a guarantor in a rental agreement. If this is the case, then know that any default on the part of the person you are guaranteeing for will not be included in your credit history. This doesn't mean you can freely be the guarantor of another person however as you'll still be responsible for their debt.

If you intend to be a guarantor or a surety, make sure to check your credit report first and contemplate whether your score can take a negative hit and that you really trust the person you are guaranteeing for. Otherwise, don't consent to being a guarantor for someone you do not completely trust.

What Happens if Your Debt Goes to Collection?

Now, there are several stages to how existing debt will be treated by a lending company. When a debt is overdue, the first thing they'd do is to try to collect it themselves. This is when you would start to get calls from representatives of the lender telling you to make payments. Usually this happens if you've been delinquent for 6 months or more.

If the primary lender gives up, the debt will be sent to a collection agency. This collection agency is hired by the primary lender to collect your debt. Hence, there is an employer-employee relationship there and if they manage to collect your debt, the collecting agency gets paid a commission.

Now – what if the collecting agency fails to get payment from you? This is when the primary lender will consider it a total loss and simply write off the debt. However, this doesn't leave you scot free! Instead, the primary lender will "sell" your debt to another party who will undertake the collection. Let's say your debt is worth 1000USD and the third party buys it for 300USD. Hence, if they collect an amount from you beyond that, they make a profit.

But really – the important question here is: how will this affect your credit score?

Well, you should understand that once you are delinquent in payments – this is already a negative score.

Chapter 7: An Overview of the Process

Let's take a quick recap. So far, we've talked about all the factors that go into credit reports, how it affects you, and even how certain relationships will affect your credit score. This should give you an overview of what your credit score is like, even if you don't have an actual copy of it yet. What we've really done in the past Chapters is to talk about the different ingredients that go into making your credit report.

Now that we've done that, we're going to talk about the cooking process and how each ingredient should be handled in order to get the perfect credit report that will give you an excellent financial reputation. This Chapter is going to be an overview of everything that's ahead of you so that you can get a full picture of the process before we dive into the specifics.

So What Happens Now? Repairing vs. Rebuilding Your Credit History
Repairing and rebuilding your credit history are two very different things. A

"repair" means there are errors on your credit history that you want to correct. Repairing often involves launching a dispute with the credit bureau.

A rebuild means that all the information in your credit history is true. It's just that you have a bad credit history – and now that you've accepted that fact, it's time to work on it.

Of course, it's perfectly possible that you have both. From here on out, this book will be guiding you through the process but first, let's look at the overview:

- Step 1: What's my credit score?

  Obviously, the first thing you should do would be to find out what's your credit score and your credit history. We already talked about the scoring system for this and what goes into your credit score, so we won't be talking about that again. In this Chapter however you will find out how and where to request your credit score.

- Step 2: Assessing your credit report.

- Step 3: Requesting records of transactions from banks, etc.

- Step 4: Disputing errors in your credit history

- Step 5: Deciding on your action on connections, joint accounts, and other relations – how will you deal with these factors?

- Step 6: Deciding on credit cards – what should you do about them?

- Step 7: Deciding on your existing loans – how do you pay off the delinquent loans that you have right now?

- Step 8: Rebuilding your credit history – how do you start paying your loans in a way that benefits your credit history?

Chapter 8: Step 1 – Ordering your Credit Report

The first step obviously concerns knowing exactly where you are starting. If you already ordered your credit report, you might wean to expand that order to other credit bureaus.

Contacting the Credit Bureaus

By now, you should know that if you want to dispute any entries in your credit history, the bureaus are the ones you should be calling. Of course, the one you contact would be the company that issues the credit report to begin with. Most people who noted an erroneous entry in their credit report will also request the report of another bureau to make sure that the error is not found anywhere else.

Here are the numbers you need to remember when contacting credit bureaus for different transactions.

Equifax
Get a Free Credit Report: You have to sign up for their online program here.
General Inquiries: 1-866-640-2273 or here.

Experian
Get a Free Credit Report: Sign up here.
General Inquiries: 1-714-830-7000 or here.

TransUnion
Get a Free Credit Report: Go to www.annualcreditreport.com
General Inquiries: 1-866-640-2273 or here.

Other Sources of Credit Report
There are other legal sources of your credit score such as consumer reporting agencies. Typically, these are the ones who provide credit scores for the purposes of property loans on residential properties. This is often paid for by you upon request. If you are getting a mortgage, you can also get a free credit score provided by the mortgage lender themselves. For purposes of personal tracking however, the top three credit bureaus would be your best choice of information.

Information You Need to Provide when Getting a Free Credit Report
As mentioned, you will be asked to provide personal information when requesting your credit report. This is as a

way to protect your own privacy and limit the number of people who see your credit history. Typically, information asked will include your Social Security number and your date of birth. Your current address will also be inquired into. People who moved within the last two years may be asked for their previous address since records aren't always up to date.

Now, aside from the Social Security Number, some of this information is easily discovered by others. This is why some credit bureaus ask for information that only you will know – such as your monthly mortgage or the interest you are currently paying on that mortgage. Each bureau will ask a different question to verify whether you are really who you say you are.

Waiting Period for a Report
Thanks to the internet, it's now possible to request your credit report online and have the results sent to you immediately. This shouldn't take more than a day or so, depending on the response time of the credit bureau.

If you opted to order a report via a call, expect to have it mailed within 15 days from the time you asked for it. The same waiting period is available if you order the report via mail, starting from the day the credit bureau received the mail. Right now, it's fairly obvious that ordering your credit report online is the better option as it gives you instant access to the information.

How Often Should You Get a Credit Report?

Since it's free, a money-wise individual should take advantage of these annual reports as often as possible. Currently, individuals can get as much as 9 free credit reports from reporting bureaus until the year 2026. Feel free to utilize 6 of those on a routine basis and leave the rest for "emergency" situations.

Unless the privilege is extended, you'll only have access to 3 free credit reports after the year 2026. Experts suggest therefore that you avail of your free credit report every 4 months, thereby allowing you to run consistent checks on your finances in the event of fraud or just to make sure that all of the information there is accurate.

Chapter 9: Step 2 – Assessing your Credit Reports

Once you have your credit report on your hands, the next step is to check it thoroughly. This is the tough part because you need to be able to have a point of reference. If you haven't been keeping up with your expenses, then you might have a hard time figuring out which transactions are correct and which ones are not. Later on, we'll talk about asking your bank for a full report on your finances so you should have a starting point once you've decided to turn your financial situation into a positive one.

Get ready by making a photocopy of the credit report you got from the credit bureau. Grab a red pen because you will be writing on the photocopy.

Personal Data
The first thing you should be looking at would be the personal information. Make sure that your name, social security number, address, and any other data is correct. Even the smallest typographical error should be taken seriously becomes this could be the gateway to identity

theft. Mark the areas that need to be corrected.

Accounts
Next up, look at the accounts that are open. The credit report will tell you if you have existing loans and their status. Look into the status of the account such as if it's close, open, when it was opened, what bank was it opened, and so on. Make sure that all the accounts attributed to your name are actually owned and used by you. Note that if you are someone's guarantor or surety, this will also be indicated in the accounts. The same is true if you have joint credit card accounts with other people.

Transactions
Once you've determined that all the accounts listed in your credit report actually belong to you, the next step is to look into the transactions. This is the part where you'll need to be more thorough and make sure that each information in there is accurate. Remember, that's 7 years of financial transactions in there so make sure to settle in for a long ride and read through the data.

There is good chance that you'll have a hard time remember some of the information there so think hard. Start from the latest data and work your way back. Make markings along the way for transactions you think are wrong or those that you don't remember anymore.

When looking through transactions – the most important thing to look for would be purchases or accounts that you did not open. If you think there is information there that you did not do – leave marks on it. Remember that transactions that happened in the past may be a bit harder to remember so try to think objectively.

Negative Information
Once you've noted that transactions that you did not do – it's time to look into the transactions that you did do. More importantly, look into the ones that have a negative impact on your credit score. This one's a bit easier to locate since the factors causing a low credit score are fairly obvious. Did you make late payments? Did you default on certain credits?

Mark these as well and pay attention to when they occurred. Again, these records will stay on your credit report for a period of 7 years. Hence, if they happened 5 or 6 years ago, you might want to just wait it out instead of actually paying up. Later on, we'll discuss this more extensively on a special Chapter.

Credit Inquiries

Look at the credit inquires you've had in the past few months. More specifically, look into the hard inquiries which are the questions made by lenders you've submitted an application to. Hard inquiries are also considered as negative information, especially if you currently have a credit ratio score of more than 30 percent.

The Score Itself

Of course, don't forget that the score itself is the final arbiter of your credit report. Take a good look at the score as well the method used to achieve it. Remember – VantageScore has a lower average of 680 while FICO has 703. Find out exactly what method is used to compute your credit score and then decide on whether it falls within your expectations.

Chapter 10: Step 3 – Requesting Information from Furnishers

Furnishers are the people or entities that provide credit bureaus with information about your financial transactions. For example, a credit card company would furnish information about you to a credit bureau which will then use this information to calculate your credit score.

Now, when tracing the accuracy of information in your credit history, there are three things to consider – your own records, the records of the furnisher, and the records of the bureau. Ideally, all three are similar. The problem happens when one of those is different from the rest and needs to be corrected. In this Chapter, we'll tackle each situation and find out what's the best approach on every matter.

Your credit report will contain information about who furnished that particular information. Is it the bank? Is it a credit card company? Is it a particular lender? Once you find out the WHO, it's time to contact that particular entity and have situation verified. Simply put, at this stage, you are merely asking the furnishing entity (FE) whether the information displayed in the credit report actually fits with the information they have about you on file.

NOTE: A large part of disputing errors is being able to identify them in the first place. It is therefore EXTREMELY important that you have kept your own records about the financial transaction. Otherwise, you might have a hard time disputing any entry on the credit report.

Difference Between Furnisher's Record and Bureau's Record

In the ordinary course of events, the information recorded by the credit bureau is similar to the information recorded by the furnisher. The question now is: what if there is a difference? Let's say that the furnisher recorded an amount of 1,520USD but for one reason or another, the numbers were transposed so that the amount reflected in the history is 5,120USD.

The best solution would be to order the financial information from the furnisher and present it to the credit bureau as your evidence. Even better is if you have your own record and could provide it to the bureau without the need for a request.

But let's say that for one reason or another, you lost your own copies of the transaction. How do you make a request to the furnisher for such information? Fortunately, this is an easy task and could be accomplished via writing or sending an online letter to the furnisher. The address of the letter depends on the location of the furnisher so make sure to check their recommended address. Sending a request via the local office is best but you can also send a similar letter to the main branch to boost priority. In many cases, an address is provided in the furnisher's website so that you know exactly where to send any question that you might have.

Again, we come to the common question: Is it better to send an online request or a written letter? Doing both is often best. But a certified written letter sent through mail is the best way for you to keep track of your request.

Difference Between your Record and the Furnisher

You would think that the difference in the information between the furnisher and the credit bureau is already your hardest problem, but not really. The real issue happens when your record of the account is widely different from that of the furnisher. If you have your own copy of the transactions, then this would be a quick fix. If not however, be prepared to have a long and tiring talk with the representatives of the furnisher. These exhausting processes should at least teach you to keep your own records of financial transactions for future use.

So what do we do now?

As a quick recap, when disputing an entry in a credit report, the credit bureau would usually send a copy of the dispute letter to the furnisher for confirmation. If the furnisher confirms the entry, then the credit bureau will decline your dispute and will tell you the reason why it was declined. If this happens, then your next step would be to go to the furnisher and present them with your evidence showing that their records are incorrect.

Remember, the credit bureau does not create your history. It only stores your credit history and leaves it as is, upon the report of the furnisher. Any error therefore can be addressed via the furnisher themselves. In most cases, disputes about furnished information requires a complete and exhaustive discussion of the loan. This will involve all the previous payments paid as well as any interests added into the principal amount. In effect there will be a complete overhaul and review of the information before determining the final output. This would then be referred to the credit bureau.

Again, this is all a matter of evidence and you should have sufficient documentation on your part to show yours is the proper one to be reported.

Chapter 11: Step 4 - Information to Submit when Disputing Specific Problems

As mentioned, it's best to send all the information you have on hand in order to avoid a frivolous ruling or rejection. The evidence you provide would be dependent on the matter you are trying to dispute. At this point, you should also understand that you should possess your own records of your financial transactions and have them attached together with the letter.

Note that all the evidence you provide should be copies only   NEVER originals.

General Attachments
Every dispute should have the following information attached. This will help speed up the process by making it easier for the credit bureau to counter check the information you provided. Keep in mind that lack of any these attachments can make your dispute frivolous:

- Your complete name, including any suffixes you might have. You can show this by putting a photocopy of a valid government ID with your full name and suffix.

- You can also send a photocopy of a valid driver's license or your passport.

- Also send your social security number. Make sure to triple check the numbers because most errors occur due to misplaced or transposed social security numbers.

- Send photocopies of any utility bills you might have which shows your address and your full name. If you changed addresses, make sure to indicate it as well as what year you resided in the particular address. Ideally you should provide your address for the past 2 years.

- Kindly make a list of the entries in your credit report that you want to dispute. This should be different from the photocopy of the credit report that you will also attach to the dispute. The photocopy of the credit report should contain markings of the items that you want to dispute. Hence, there will be 2 documents that show alleged errors in your credit history.

The next thing to address would be these specific disputes that you have against the report and how you can prove that their records are erroneous. Now this is a simple matter if what you are trying to dispute is personal information. For example, if there is something wrong with your address or your name is misspelled, it's easy enough to send and ID showing the true information. Do not ignore these small clerical errors because identity theft is a strong possibility in the United States.

The problem happens if the error is more complicated. For example, what would you do if the credit report shows that you have an account with a particular creditor when you never opened such account? How do you prove a negative?

In this chapter we will talk about the best evidence you can provide when confronted with complicated issues in your credit report.

I did not open this account.
Let's say your credit report show that you have opened a credit account with XYZ bank. In order to dispute this particular

issue, you would need a statement from XYZ bank saying that you have not and have never opened a credit line in any of their branches. You can request this kind of information from the bank itself and send a photocopy of the letter with your dispute. Remember that you should always send a copy to the bureau so that you can keep the original in your personal file. This will help you in the event that the dispute goes to court and you need to provide evidence in your behalf.

This is not my information
This covers anything and everything connected with your personal identification. This includes your Social Security Number, your address or past addresses, your mobile phone number, and any other data that might be there but is incorrectly attributed to you. It doesn't matter how small it is because incorrect information can make it easy for identity theft to occur. Even small clerical errors should be noted and corrected.

This account is already closed.
If a close account is still present in your credit history, the simplest way to deal

with it is by showing a letter from the bank. Again, you will request a letter from the bank stating that the account under your name with number ABCDE has been closed on a specific date.

Note that this dispute will only close the account but not delete the transactions you made under the same account. For example, you have a credit card that you already closed on December 2018. Transactions you made on the card for 2017 and before that would still be present on your credit history. Hence, if you made late payments on that account then this would still be a factor for computing credit score.

This error often occurs when it comes to joint accounts of couples. If you've gone through a recent divorce and want to make sure that previous joint accounts haven't ruined your credit score, confirming that the joint account is listed as closed can improve the accuracy of the score.

This debt is listed more than once.
When making this claim, make sure that you've attached a copy of the credit report with the double entries clearly

marked. Having a copy of the bank's report should bolster your claim when attached with the dispute. This is a more common error than you think and if listed twice upon payment, there is a chance that the extra one will remain and be tagged as delinquent.

The balance or credit limit is incorrect
Any error in your balance or credit limit can change your debt-to-credit-ratio. Computing this amount is fairly simple and most credit reports will provide a list of credit limits and outstanding debts for quick comparison. The typical problem here occurs when you've made late payments that is not yet recorded or reported by the bank or other lending institution. Updates on credit transactions are not done on a daily basis and therefore takes some time before it is reflected on your report.

The best way to handle this is by waiting a few months and ordering your credit score again. In the interval, you can also try updating your account with the furnisher to serve as your personal record of the transaction.

Inaccurate dates

Dates are very important when it comes to credit reports because they can indicate late payments. For example, you are supposed to make monthly payments on or before the 15th day of the month. If the record erroneously shows that payment was made on the 16th day, then this will be logged in as a late payment. Remember, that your credit score is computed not just on the basis of whether or not you paid but also on whether or not you paid on time. Therefore, even the smallest discrepancy in terms of timeliness of your payment should be disputed.

How do you dispute this particular error? Having your own record of when payment was made is the best possible evidence that can be provided. You can attach a copy of your deposit slip or any other document evidencing that payment was made on that particular date.

I am only a co-signor
A co-signor simply means that you are the guarantor or the surety of a particular debt. When entering into this kind of transaction, the principal debtor is the one who should be paying the amount. Therefore, co-signing should only be

included in your credit report if the principal debtor fails to make payment.

So when should you launch a dispute over this? Ideally, you know when the debt was signed and the date of its maturity. If the co-signed loan appears on your credit report before its maturity, then a dispute is proper. You can send a letter to the credit bureau stating that you are merely a co-signor and that the amount is not yet demandable. An attachment of a copy of the document should also be included in the letter.

This is old information that should be removed now.
Keep in mind that credit information only has a lifespan of 7 years or if there is a declaration of bankruptcy – it should only be there for 10 years. Hence, do not be afraid to launch a dispute with respect to the propriety of the credit being listed in the history. If you know for a fact that the information was 7 or 10 years ago, as the case may be, then have it removed from the report. You can attach a copy of the debt or late payment, showing when the transaction was made with a statement that it is beyond the 7-year coverage of the report.

Chapter 12: Step 5 – Launching a Dispute on your Credit Report

Disputing a credit report is advisable if, after ordering your credit information, you've noted that there are marked inconsistencies. Perhaps debt that's already paid is still indicated there as unpaid or perhaps there have been monthly payments that are not reflected on the credit report.

Common Credit Report Errors

The only way you can figure out the errors in a credit report is by comparing it with your own records. This being the case, it stands to reason that you need to maintain a record of all transactions you've have with the bank or any lender. If you've made payments, there should be a deposit slip showing payment was made. If there was an agreement to defer payment, it should be expressed in writing.

Here are the typical errors in credit reports that you might want to look into:

- Errors in identity information such as the wrong name, the wrong address or the wrong phone number. This is important since your credit information could be the subject of identity theft. You want to make sure that should there be any questions made regarding your financial transactions, they would be contacting the right person via your address or your phone number.

- Look for mixed files or mixed information. This happens when you have the same name with another customer, creating a mixture of financial information due to the confusion. This happens more often than you might think and could even occur from the banks.

- Existing accounts under your name that you do not remember getting or do not remember opening. This can be a sign of identity theft and should be removed from your record as soon as possible.

- Look for accounts that are already closed but are still noted as open by the credit bureau.

- Incorrect designations on an account. For example, you are listed there as the account owner when in truth, you are simply an authorized user of the account. This happens often for credit cards issued in favor of a family member and is extended to other members.

- A paid-off delinquency such as when you have late payments that are eventually paid off. Note that there is a huge distinction here between unpaid late fees and paid late ones. A late payment will always be on record even if it is already paid. What you need to correct is if payment was already made but it is still "unpaid" on the record.
- Single debts are listed more than once in the record.
- Incorrect balances on the record
- Credit limits are incorrect

Here's the Sample Letter for Disputes

After identifying the errors on the report or the bank, you can now pen a letter telling them about the dispute. Fortunately, there is a sample dispute letter suggested by the FTC with a pattern that you can easily follow. The letter should also contain the errors to be corrected, the corrections you want made, and the evidence you have in support of your request. You will then end the letter by stating the action you want the bureau or bank to make – such as you want correction or deletion of the entry.

The address of the bureau where this letter should be sent is available below. As for the FE, ask your local brand about where the letter must be delivered for appropriate action to be taken. Important – do not simply give the letter to an officer of the bank without asking for a proof of receipt. Have someone from the bank draft a letter signifying that they received your letter in their capacity as an employee of the bank, have them sign it, and then make sure it is dated.

Make Multiple Copies of Your Evidence

Most people make the mistake of sending the originals or not making enough copies of the documents they're using as evidence. If you are going to send evidentiary document, make sure you also make copies for yourself – even if you have the originals. Hence, compile one set of copies for the bureau, one set of copies for the bank, one set of copies for yourself, and keep the originals somewhere safe. It is also recommended that you make a copy of your credit report and place a line or circles on the portions you want to be corrected.

So What Exactly Do You Send the Bureau?

Just a quick recap, here's what your envelope to the bureau or FE should contain:

- The letter as provided by the FTC
- The COPIES of your evidence – we'll discuss more of this later as to what kind of evidence should you be sending exactly.
- The COPY of the credit report along with notations or markings showing where corrections needs to be made. If there are several of those problems, you can try marking each correction as A, B, C, D, or any other identifying marker so as not to cause confusion during checking.

Sending your Dispute via Letter

For physical letters sent to credit bureaus, online forms can be downloaded, printed, and filled out before sending it to them. Attach a letter with the form and make sure to follow the instructions for sending. Link for the instructions is also provided below.

Equifax
Link to online dispute form.
Link to instructions for Equifax.
Mail To:
Equifax Information Services, LLC
PO Box 740256
Atlanta, GA 30374-0256

TransUnion
Link to online dispute form.
Link to instructions for TransUnion.
Mail To:
TransUnion Consumer Solutions

P.O. Box 2000
Chester, PA 19016-2000

Experian
Link to online dispute form.
Link to instructions for Experia.
Mail To:
Experian
P.O. Box 4500
Allen, TX 75013

Disputes Via Online Letter
You can also send a dispute letter via email by following the steps provided by the credit bureau on their website. The pattern previously provided would also

work for this. You can scan the documents you want to attach and send them as one PDF file to help with checking.

Which One is Better?
The question of which is better between the physical letter and the online form depends on how quickly you need the results. An online application will give you a quicker response – but the mail would offer better tracking on your part. It serves as an excellent paper trail, especially if you send it via Certified Mail.

Investigation Process
Once the letter has been sent, you now have to give the recipient's time to respond to it. This takes about 30 days from the time the bureau receives the letter but would often be shorter. Now, you'll have to be patient about this because the process doesn't just stop with the Credit Bureau. For example, if they receive a dispute letter from you, they're going to investigate that by sending a letter to the entity that provided the information.

Hence, let's say you are disputing an error from XYZ Bank. The Credit Bureau would send a letter to XYZ Bank who would then investigate the same and respond to the Bureau. This is why it's important to send your dispute letter both to the Credit Bureau and to the Bank, therefore making sure that the respective entities will give proper attention to your plea.

Now, if the bank made a simple error – the buck stops there. A correction will be made, and you'll have your Credit Report corrected. However – what if the bank itself has a problem with their records?

Frivolous Errors
Note that these requests for correction or disputes won't always be addressed. Within the 30-day period, the Credit Bureau may choose to send you a letter declining the request because it is a "frivolous error. A frivolous error is one that's considered unimportant or not something that would really impact your credit score. If you send insufficient information to make it possible for the bureau to check your dispute, then it might be dismissed for being frivolous. Understand however that personal information – even a clerical one –

should be disputed as you do not want to leave the window open for identity theft.

The Follow Up – Possible Results

So after sending your dispute letter, several things might happen. First, they might recognize the error and make the necessary changes. Second, they might reject the dispute and claim that their records are true and correct. Third – they might argue that the dispute is frivolous. There is also a fourth option – the credit bureau may not respond at all. Your next step would depend primarily on what the Credit Bureau does as a response to your action.

Dispute is Allowed

If the dispute is allowed, that's good news for you! The bureau will inform you in writing about their decision. Once this happens, the next step is to ask the Bureau to inform third parties about this particular change in your credit score. This refers to the people to whom they furnished the credit information such as your bank, the insurance company, or your prospective landlord. In fact, you'll even get a free copy of the report in case you are right, and a change was made to the history because of your report.

Dispute is Rejected

Now, it's also quite possible that the dispute will be rejected. Perhaps the bank which furnished the information continues to report the disputed data. If this happens, you can ask the credit bureau to attach a copy of the dispute to your credit report and furnish it together with the score each time it is requested by a third party in the future. Hence, if someone asks for your credit report, they'll also get a copy of the dispute telling your side of the story. This gives the third party a chance to take your side into consideration before entering into a transaction with you.

Dispute is Considered Frivolous

Once the dispute is considered frivolous, the credit bureau will inform you in writing. Now, what situations will fall under a frivolous claim? There are several possible reasons. The first is if you failed to provide sufficient information in your initial letter. This is why it's important to attach all the relevant information into the letter before sending it. This way, it speeds up the process and gives you the exact results you need within the 30-day time frame.

Another possible reason for the dispute's rejection based on frivolity is if you launched an identical dispute in the past that was rejected for valid reasons. If the credit bureau believes that the previous dispute has been properly handled, then they won't expend resources to investigate a new one which has basically the same grounds.

Do NOT Dispute Negative Information

One thing you should keep in mind is that disputes are meant to correct wrong information. If you launch a dispute simply because it doesn't look good on your account, then it will instantly be rejected by the credit bureau. Worse, you might be flagged down and all future disputes you send might be taken with a grain of salt. It's a lot like the boy who cried wolf – and you don't want that, especially considering the importance of having accurate credit score. Hence, launch a dispute only when you honestly believe there is an error there that needs to be corrected. Otherwise, the only way this negative report will be gone from your credit history is through time.

What if the Credit Bureau Refuses to Change the Information?

If the credit bureau doesn't want to change the information on your credit report despite providing evidence on the matter, you can take more drastic actions to get the results you want. Now, there are several options available and it's best to try the less-harsh methods first before going nuclear:

Contact the Creditor

Ideally, the credit bureau would consult with the creditor before admitting or rejecting the matter for dispute. If rejection occurs, you have the option of going directly to the creditor and demand from them the removal of concerned data. This can be done through a letter like this or you can create your own.

Now, the creditor may choose to agree or disagree with you. If they do, then a positive letter sent by the creditor can be copied and furnished to the credit bureau. If not however, you can escalate the matter to the higher management of the creditor such as the President or the

CEO. Note that if you are going to do this, you'll have to present more information or evidence to support your cause.

Refile the Dispute
You can also file the dispute again, this time with more information attached to support your position. This is a good option if the credit bureau responds with a statement saying that there is not enough data in their system to believe your argument. Simply refiling the dispute without any additional information will make your case seem frivolous and actually make it harder for you to gain their attention.

File with the CFPB
Another option is to file a complaint directly with the Consumer Financial Protection Bureau. This is a good move if you think that there was unfairness in the process and that a valid error exists. Once the CFPB gets your letter, they are compelled to respond in a period of 15 days. The CFPB will merely act as your agent in that they will contact the agency on your behalf. Since they're a government agency, they'll have more clout and be able to elicit a clearer answer from the Credit Bureau. If this action

proves futile, the CFPB may also choose to send your information to another agency who can provide you further help.

File a Complaint Against the Creditor
Credit companies also make mistakes but may not always be willing to accept it. If a request is not enough for them to launch a proper investigation, then you have the option of filing a direct complaint with the Federal Trade Commission or the FTC or the CFPB. The overseeing agencies typically vary depending on the type of creditor you are trying to complain about, but the receiving agency should be able to forward the complaint to the proper entities concerned. While these agencies won't represent you in a lawsuit, they are capable of launching a complaint into the operations of the creditor if there are enough issues submitted by users.

State Consumer Protection Agency Complaints
Depending on the state, your state attorney general or consumer protection agency should be able to offer some assistance during this problem. Send a complaint through your state attorney general and they'd be able to shed more

light on the applicable credit laws in your State.

Congressional Representative or Senator
In some instances, writing to your representative or senator can also improve your standing. At the very least, your senator could review the laws being enforced with respect to credit and make changes if they find that there are any gaps or lapses on the law itself or its enforcement.

Sue the Creditor or Credit Reporting Agency
If there were serious harm on your part, you can sue the agency you believe to be responsible for the problem. Under the Fair Credit Reporting Act, you have the right to sue the credit reporting agency if there is willful or negligent noncompliance with your request. Understand that this right to sue is limited by time. You can only file a suit within two years after discovery of their non-compliance or within five years after the harmful behavior happens. The creditor or furnisher may also be used but this is a more complicated process.

Freezing Your Credit
You can also have your credit frozen via any of these credit bureaus. This is advisable if you think you are the victim of identity theft or you think you are going to be vulnerable to one. Now, there are three possible ways to have your credit frozen: online, by phone, or through mail. Of the three, the online and phone options are best if time is of the essence for you.

Equifax
Online: Click here.
Phone: 888-298-0045
Mail:
Equifax Information Services, LLC
P.O. Box 105788
Atlanta, GA 30348

TransUnion
Online: Click here.
Phone: 888-909-8872
Mail:
TransUnion
P.O. Box 160
Woodlyn, PA 19094

Experian

Online: Click here.
Phone: 888-397-3742
Mail:
Experian Security Freeze
P.O. Box 9554
Allen, TX 75013

Chapter 13: Step 6 - Deciding on Action for Connections, Joint Accounts, and other Relations

We already talked about relationships and connections affecting your credit score. These are the relationships that could pull your credit score downwards even without any action on your part. For example, if you own a joint account with your sister, any purchase made by her on that credit card and remains unpaid at the end of the month will be recorded in your credit history. Therefore, you want to make sure that any loan under your name whether or not someone else made the actual purchase, has been paid. This is because the credit bureau will not divide the score between the two of you. Instead, it will assume that the loan is attributed only to one person hence, in the given example, even your sister will have the same negative mark in her credit history.

So how do you fix this problem? In this particular chapter we will talk about the different relationships that could pull your credit history down and how to fix each one.

Joint Account

With joint accounts the best option is to simply cancel the account. This is especially true if you hold a joint account with someone who does not pay their bill or who makes excessive purchases. Keep in mind however, that closing the account will not remove the late payments or unpaid debt in the credit history. This will only prevent further debts made on the specific account. The late payments will remain on your credit history unless they are paid off or after 7 years whichever comes first.

Another good option is to talk to the other person and have the debts paid. You can have an agreement with respect to how credits will be paid so that there will be no negative marks on your credit history. One thing you should keep in mind, however, is that the credit card company is not bound by this agreement. Hence, even there is an agreement between the two of you, and yet the debt remains unpaid, you cannot tell the credit card company that the other person is the one who should be paying. You also cannot use this agreement to contest the negative marks on your credit history. This private agreement can only help you when getting back the amount you paid on behalf of the other person.

To illustrate, let's say that you have a joint account with someone and there is an agreement that you would each pay for the purchases you've made on that account. You have that on writing and appropriately signed. Unfortunately, the other person doesn't hold up their end of the deal, so you have to pay for their purchases. Once you've done this, you can go launch a suit against that person in order to claim back what they owe, using the document as proof.

Finally, there is also the option of not opening a joint account at all. Of course, this maybe a bit too late for you if you are reading this particular book. The only thing you have to remember is that from here on out you should not open a joint account with anyone that you cannot completely trust on a financial aspect.

Protect your Credit through Proper Closure of Joint Accounts
In the interest of making sure your credit score remains in good standing when closing a joint account, we'll proceed to talk about how to properly get this done.

As already mentioned, you don't need the approval of the co-account holder to close a common account. However, it's important that you inform them of this decision and make provisions as to how the unpaid amount shall be paid. If you want to speed up the process, you'll have to make the payment yourself.

Here's what you need to do when closing a joint credit card account:

- Start by redeeming any unused rewards to make the most out of the credit card before you cancel the same.
- Make sure to pay the credit card completely before cancelling it. The credit card company will not let you close the account if the balance of the card is not zero.
- Once the card balance hits zero, write a certified letter to your credit card company requesting that the account be closed. Make sure to keep a receipt of the certified mail as this will be your proof that a letter has been set.
- Most people will tell you that closing the credit card is best done through a call. This is also possible – but discouraged when done alone. Hence,

if you are going to close your credit card account – do it in writing and follow it up with a phone call. This way, the credit card company will focus their attention on your request.

- Wait for a confirmation of credit card cancellation. One thing you should keep in mind here is that the notice of cancellation should be done in writing. If they call you to say that the account has been closed, ask them to send a letter stating the same information. This is an added security on your part and can help prevent the chances of identity theft.

- Two months after the confirmed cancellation, ask for copies of your credit report from all three bureaus. The new credit report should reflect that the account has been closed. Note that it will only indicate closure – but the history that comes with that account will stay there. Hence, if you made a late payment on that account two years ago, it will still be stated in the history and thus will form part of your credit score.

Guarantors and Sureties

Being someone's guarantor or surety means that you become responsible for their debts if it remains unpaid at the end of the term of the loan. If this happens, the only way for the negative mark to disappear is if you paid the loan yourself or you compel the primary lender to make the payment. Of course, you can also wait for the seven years that it will take for the non-payment to disappear from your credit history.

The question is can you cancel a contract of suretyship or guaranty? The strict answer is NO. Once you enter into this contract the only way it could be canceled is if payment is made. But could you replace yourself in the contract? This would depend on the lender and the existing law in your location.

This is because the personal circumstances of the guarantor or surety is also considered by the lender when approving a loan by the primary borrower. For example, if the guarantor or surety does not have a stable income or also has a bad credit score then chances are the loan will still be denied. In fact, the primary reason why people with bad credit scores seek a guarantor or a surety is to improve their chances of being approved by the lender.

So, let's say you want to remove yourself from the contract of guaranty or surety while the loan is still not demandable. If this is the case, then a new guarantor or surety must take your place. This new guarantor or surety must be approved by the lender, otherwise you cannot be removed from the contract.

Hence, it can really be hard to improve your credit score if you are in this kind of transaction. The best way to handle this would be to not enter into a contract at all. If your primary goal is to simply improve your credit score, you can also pay off the debt yourself and then launch an action against the primary borrower so that they can refund what you spent. This might take longer and can decrease your savings, but this would be the best option for your credit score.

Credit Score and Marriage
The good news is your credit score is not affected by your marriage. The husband and wife have individual credit scores and one will not affect the other. The only exception to this is if you have a joint

credit card account which will be reflected on both your credit histories. Since we already talked about that there is no need to explain further. Keep in mind however, that the credit report of your spouse can still affect any loans you might choose to take in the future.

For example, if you are taking out a home mortgage as a couple the lender would actually take both of your credit score into consideration before choosing to reject or accept your application. In most cases, the lender will accept the application but impose a high interest rate on it. Think of it as averaging your grade in school; if most subjects have very high scores but one has a failing grade, this failing grade will pull down your average. This is the same principle followed by banks when lending to spouses.

So how can you fix this problem? There are 2 possible approaches, first is by delaying the loan and simply focusing on the improvement of the bad credit score. Once it has been improved, you can apply for a mortgage loan and hopefully get the interest rate that you want. The next option is to get the loan under the name of the person with the better credit score. This will marginally improve the interest rate as opposed to the interest rate given to a couple.

Collecting Agency and Debt

If your debt goes to a collecting agency this is as far as it gets. The loan is unpaid and will be reflected in your credit history until it has been paid or after the seven years is up. Your action would depend on how long the credit has been unpaid. For example, if the amount is 6 years ago, then you might as well wait for the period to lapse. If it is a fairly recent unpaid debt however, it would be best to pay it off so that it does not cause a negative mark to your credit score. Understand that when it comes to credit scores, the most recent debts weigh heavier so really, you can pay off these delinquent debts later on focus on the ones that are just a few weeks or months old.

Chapter 14: Step 7 - Deciding on Credit Cards

In this Chapter, we're going to talk about your credit card and what should be done with it when trying to improve your credit score. Think of your credit cards as the faucet that facilitates the flow of debt. Before addressing the debts themselves, you first need to figure out if you to actually have all those faucets operational or perhaps cut off a few to help you better manage the flow.

Credit cards make up most of a person's credit history. The average American owns 4 credit cards at any given time. As we already mentioned it is usually not a good idea to close a credit card because this will negativcly impact your debt to credit ratio. However, some credit cards are better left closed because holding them for the long term can do more harm to your financial circumstances even if they do help with your credit score.

Addressing Conflicts of Interest

One thing I want you to remember when reading this book is that your credit score and your financial stability are two completely different things. Just because you have a good credit score, it doesn't mean that you are financially secured. Remember a credit score will only impact future debts you might choose to have.

To illustrate let's say that you have a credit card for ten years. Unfortunately, this credit card has a very high interest rate. Closing it will help you save on monthly expenses especially since you can get a new card with a much lower interest rate. Unfortunately, closing this old card would also mean that your average credit history will decrease. As we already discussed, credit history is a factor while computing a credit score. Ideally, a longer credit history would be better for your report.

So there is a conflict here. Should you keep the ten-year credit card with a high interest rate and maintain a good credit score? Or should you open a new account with a low interest rate but negatively impact your credit score.

The best answer here is to close the ten-year credit card. This way you can save up on expenses by reducing the interest rate you pay every month. While this might be bad for your credit score now, it can help your future financial transactions, add to your savings, and make it easier for you to build your credit. Simply put when given the choice, always make the decision for future financial stability.

If you must, grab a piece of pen and paper and do the math before making this decision.

Closing Unused Credit Cards DO NOT Improve your Credit Score

Let's say you have 5 credit cards, each one having a credit limit of $10,000 which means that overall, you can borrow a total of $50,000. You have debt on 4 out of these 5 cards costing at $1,000 each – which means that you have a total debt of $4,000. Your debt to credit ratio is $4,000:$50,000 or a percentage of 8 percent.

Now let's say you decide to close one credit card because you are not using it. There is no debt on it so why not? Now, your debt credit ratio is $4,000:$40,000. Do you see the difference now? The new percentage is 10% and that's not a good increase.

Hence, if you have an unused credit card and it's not costing you anything, just leave it be. This will actually be a positive thing towards your credit score.

Credits Cards that are OK to Close

Of course, some credit cards when closed, can actually help improve your credit score. It's just a question of exactly what kind of credit card needs to be closed and paid off as well as WHEN it should be done.

Joint Accounts After Separation or Divorce

As mentioned, marriage doesn't mean you and your spouse would share a credit score. However, if you do own a joint credit card – then this information will appear on both your credit history and will be factored individually.

This being the case, if your relationship ends – such as when there is divorce or separation, it's best to have the joint account cancelled completely. This is more of a preventive measure than anything else. A separation – no matter how friendly it is, can cause negative emotions on both sides. Hence, it's likely that one spouse or the other will choose to purchase using the joint credit card, impacting your score and placing a financial burden on you.

In many cases, the joint account is also used to purchase items in relation to the marriage. For example, the account could be used for vacations, for home furniture, for support, and so on. Simply put – the main purpose for opening the account is gone and it is therefore necessary to close the account itself.

Here's an interesting question though – can you close a joint account without the approval of the other person? Yes – as long as you are one of the account holders, the bank or Credit Card Company will not require the agreement of the other person. Note that this may vary from one lender to the next.

Annual Fees are Too High
Sometimes, it's better to close an account if it demands a high maintaining fee, even if you have no payables on it. Remember what we said about debt to credit ratio? The general rule is that you should not close an unused account. However, there are exceptions to this

rule such as when the credit card has a high annual fee. Note – we're talking about annual fee here and NOT interest rate. Interest rates do not accumulate if there is no remaining debt in the account.

An annual fee however is a different discussion. This occurs whether or not you have an existing unpaid balance on the credit card. If the annual fee is too high and does not justify keeping the account open – then you can always call the credit card company to close it down.

Understand that this is a judgment call on your part. While a credit card may have a high annual fee, it might also come with additional perks that you like. For example, it could provide you with flight points for travel or it could offer you discounted access to favorite services. Make sure to weigh the pros and cons of opening a new account and try to figure out if the side perks are worth paying the annual fee for. Borrowers of good standing may also ask the credit card company to waive the annual fee, but this means that you'll be using the credit card when buying items.

Buying Habit

If you are constantly tempted by the fact that you have a credit card that's not maxed out – closing it might be the better choice as opposed to a situation where you borrow more than you are capable of paying off in the future. Closing the credit card is at least a good way to control your spending habits once you've already done all other techniques to curb you desire to buy.

Opening a New Credit Card
Some people would say that the last thing you want to do if you have a bad credit score is to open a new credit card. This is mostly true since the interest rate on this credit card will be computed based on your existing credit score. Some entities however provide credit cards specifically for people with bad credit scores. These companies take your unique situation in hand and actually provide you with an interest rate that's designed to help instead of making things harder for you.

Here are good examples of these credit cards as of this writing. Note that many of these cards are secured credit cards. This means that you'll be required to maintain an account with the bank or the credit card company as a security deposit. This security deposit is typically the same value as the limit of your credit card.

Discover It Secured

This secured card offers its holders rewards, allowing you to enjoy certain perks if you pay your bills on time. The real unique feature of this however is from a secured card, you can upgrade to an unsecured card upon review. The review process is automatically done when you are already building a good credit history with their card so that you'll be rewarded by no longer needing a security deposit.

OpenSky Secured Visa Credit Card

This card doesn't perform a credit check when accepting your application. The credit card company simply requires you to pay annual fees for the service. Even better, you don't need to have a bank account in order to have this one. So how do you fund your secured credit card? The security deposit is made through money order or via Western Union payment. The payment of bills is done in the same way.

Capital One Secured Mastercard

The great thing about this secured card is that you don't have to pay the full amount of your credit limit. Instead, you only need to pay a smaller amount as a security – making it perfect for people who do not have cash on hand. With Capital One, you can get a credit line of around 200USD using a deposit of just 99USD. On time payments will also earn you additional credit limits even without depositing more.

DCU Visa Platinum Secured Credit Card
This particular card comes with some of the lowest interest rates in the market today, even for someone who has bad credit. Note though that in order to get this card, you need to be a member of the Digital Credit Union which costs around 10USD.

Credit Builder Secured Visa Credit Card
As the name suggests, this credit building card gives users the opportunity to improve their credit score through adjustable credit limits. If you pay on time, the credit limit can be increased so that you can also improve the debt to credit ratio of your score. Note though that you also have to make further deposits to increase your credit limit, but

this can be done gradually. You can get this card from Armed Forces Bank.

Harley Davidson Visa Secured Card
If what you want is a card that doesn't charge an annual fee, this is the best one to get. Those who have Harley Davidson products can also get rewards related to the brand.

Of course, those are just few of the credit cards specially made for people with bad credit scores. If you scan the market, you'll find that there are dozens of those that can be perfect for your use.

Judgment Call on Closing a Credit Card

We previously talked about credit cards and how it's better to leave it open as opposed to closing it and reducing the amount you are allowed to borrow. We also talked about the situation when closing the credit card would be better as opposed to keeping it open. So let's say that you arrived at the decision that there is no other option but to close one of your credit card accounts. You have a hard time resisting temptation, so the next best thing is to close the account – what account do you choose?

You would think that cutting the one with the highest interest rate would be best – but if a good credit score is your ultimate goal, this should be carefully balanced with other considerations.

For example, credit history is a huge factor when computing credit scores. If you have a long credit history on a specific card, then this would be seen as a positive sign. Hence, let's say you have 3 cards – one you've had for 5 years, a second one you've had for 3 years and another one you've had only for 1 year. The 5 years has an interest rate of 5 percent, the 3 years has an interest rate of 8 percent and the 1 year has an interest rate of 5 percent too. If you close the 5-year card, you'll have an average history of 2. However, if you close the 1-year card, the average history would be 4. If you choose to close the one with the highest interest rate, your average history would be 3 years.

So which one would be the best choice? With just a single difference, it would be better to close the card with the highest interest rate. However, if all three actually come with the same interest rate of five percent – do not hesitate and just close the account with the shortest history.

If you can do the math about this, that would be perfect. Just calculate how much you spend on the card in terms of interest and make a judgment call. At this point, please keep in mind that wise financial decisions should be considered long-term. For example, even if you own a credit card for 10 years – if it's costing you massively in terms of interest rate, then your credit history is worth sacrificing so that you can use your money better.

Chapter 15: Step 8 – Prioritizing your Existing Loans

What we've done so far is to determine your credit limit and find out how much debt you have in relation to the credit limit. This is essentially what debt-to-credit ratio is all about. In the previous chapter, we made a discussion as to how credit cards should be handled. Should we close it? Or keep it open. Keep in mind that closing a credit card may be the better decision in the long run even if it means that your credit score will suffer in the meantime.

In this chapter, we will discuss your existing loans and how to properly handle it. If you really want to improve your credit score, then you'll have to resign yourself to the fact that you have to make payments on your debts. The problem here is that while you may want to pay off your debts, you may not have the financial capacity to do this. Or perhaps even if you do have the money, you want to pay off the debts that will have the quickest positive impact on your life. Here are some things you should note if you want to pay debts with credit score improvement in mind.

Is it Old or New Credit?

Remember what we said about your credit history going only as far as 7 years? The age of your debt will determine if repaying it is worth the trouble. An old debt that has gone to collections could actually be reactivated if you choose to settle it with the credit card company. The problem here is that the reactivated debt could be logged in as a new debt, thereby pulling your credit score downwards. Unfortunately, you do not have any control on how an old debt will be recognized when reactivated. This is completely up to the furnisher on how the credit will be reported to the bureau. So how do you go about this problem?

A principle you should remember is that "new trumps old". This means that your old debts will have more negative impact on your credit score as opposed to all debts. Hence, if you want to lift your credit score quickly, a targeted approach on the newest debts would be your best course of action. That being the case, first pay off the most recent delinquent debts listed on your credit history. From here

work your way back until you are
comfortable with your credit score. Note
that this is a balancing act because even
as you pay remaining debts in your credit
history, you also have to pay future debts
that you may incur as part of your day to
day life.

Options for Repaying Credit Card Debt

So let's say that you want to pay off your
debt but do not have the amount needed
to have a zero balance on the account.
Does this mean that you just stop paying
altogether? Of course not. Many credit
card companies are open to alternative
modes of payment with their borrowers.
In most cases, they simply want to get
back as much money as possible in order
to remain operational. Therefore, it's
perfectly possible for you to contact them
and propose ways to pay off the debt in a
more budget-friendly manner.

Here are the typical options that you can
propose to a credit card company:

Lump-sum Settlement
If you have a large chunk of money, you
can actually use this to pay off an existing
debt and wipe it completely off your

credit history. The problem here is what if your chunk of money is less than what you actually owe? Again, many credit card companies are open to negotiation. There is a very good chance that they will lower the overall payable amount if you will pay it off in cash. This is especially true if a large part of the debt is simply accumulated interest rate.

What you have to remember when choosing this settlement is that your letter to the credit card company has to be clear as to what is being paid by the lump-sum payment. It has to be stated there that the lump-sum payment is the full payment for all outstanding debts including and up to the interest rate. You also have to make sure that your request, if approved, is given to you in writing. Make sure to store this so that any dispute you may have about the account can be easily solved with this letter.

You also have to be careful about what is known as a "charge off". A charge off is a situation wherein the credit company will wipe off the debt from their accounting books but does not wipe off your obligation. This is actually worse for you because what this only does is balance the accounts of the lender. It is simply an accounting correction with the debt still remaining and recorded in your credit history. Hence, if you are looking for a lump-sum settlement, there must be a categorical acceptance of the payment as a way to completely wipe off the debt. In your letter to the credit card company, make sure that you also requested that they report the payment to the credit bureaus.

In most cases, the lender will forgive any unpaid debt in excess of what you paid in lump-sum settlement. For example, if you owe the credit card company 1000USD and manage to settle on 700USD as full payment, the credit card company will mark the unpaid amount of 300USD as "forgiven" debt. This will be seen as an income by the government and therefore be part of the income taxes you have to pay for the year it was forgiven. Can you do anything about this? Not really, the recording of forgiven debt is an accounting requirement and is not something that the credit card company can choose to ignore.

Workout Arrangement

A workout arrangement is a situation where you will be asking the bank or credit card company to lower your interest rate and your minimum monthly payment. What happens here is that you will claim failure to make future payments on the account. Therefore, the bank will respond by first: cutting the credit line, and then adjusting your minimum payments to fit with your current financial capacity.

Here's the problem with this arrangement: when the bank or Credit Card Company cuts your line, this will raise your credit utilization ratio. Hence, you will still owe the same amount but your total capacity to borrow will decrease. As already mentioned, a high credit utilization ratio will negatively impact your credit score.

So why choose this credit settlement option? This is really a long running game plan on your part. Even if your credit score suffers with this particular decision, you will be able to gain back on it as you pay off the debt faster.

Forbearance Program

The forbearance program is a lot like the workout program. The main difference between these two is that the forbearance program is temporary. What happens is that the lender will adjust your interest rate and minimum monthly payments for a specified and limited amount of time. There is an expectation that things will go back to normal and that you will be able to return to the original agreement after such time. A good example of this is what happened in 2020 during the corona virus pandemic. Business owners or private individuals who have lost their income during lockdown but expect to gain it back once the lockdown is lifted can ask a forbearance program from the lenders.

So how will this affect your credit score? Since the forbearancc program does not come with any forgiveness, there won't be a negative impact on your credit history. You will still pay the total amount of the debt including the interest albeit the period for payment will be longer.

Debt Management Program
The debt management program includes the participation of a third party. What

they will do is talk to all your creditors and essentially unify the overall debt so that you will be making singular payments. To illustrate, you owe Creditor A 5000USD, you owe Creditor B 3000USD, and you owe Creditor C 2000USD. Now let's say that Creditor A requires an interest rate of 3% per month, Creditor B on the other hand wants 4% per month, and Creditor C requires payments 5% per months.

Debt management will add up all these debts totaling 10000USD and negotiate with your lender to have a unified interest. For example, the 10000USD debt will only have a credit interest of 3%. This will make the debt more manageable on your part because you only have to pay one lender and pay only a lowered interest rate of 3%.

Here's the catch though: debt management companies are private entities that also require payment. You have the option of choosing non-profit organizations if you are unable to secure the services of a private company. There are several non-profit organizations, but you can start with the National Foundation for Credit Counseling. There is also the Association of Independent Consumer Credit Counseling Agencies.

Going back on credit score, how will debt management affect your credit score? Since you will be paying off the full debt, even with a lowered interest rate, this preference for debt management will not substantially hurt your credit score.

Debt Settlement Program

Debt settlement program is the last choice if nothing else works. There are 2 ways to do this, first is if you contact your credit card company yourself and ask for lower payments. In this situation, you will stop paying all your debts until you come to an agreement about lowered payments. Obviously, this will hurt your credit score because stopping any payment, despite pending application, will negatively impact your score. Keep in mind that paying even smaller amounts is better than paying nothing at all. This is different from debt management because you will not be paying the full amount of the debt. More importantly, there is no unification with debt settlement. Instead, you will be talking to the lenders one-by-one in order to settle the outstanding balance. If you have more than one lender, this can be a very difficult and long process.

The second option for debt settlement would be finding profit-oriented debt Settlement Company. What happens here is that debt Settlement Company will pay off the debt to the lender and then require payments from you. Simply put there will be a change of creditor and all of the payments will be directed to the private entity. The catch here is that the private entity would also ask for payment on top of the debt.

For example, you owe the credit card company 1000USD. The credit settlement company talks with the credit card company and manages to lower the payable amount to 800$. The settlement company will now pay 800$ and wipe off your debt. In return however, you will have to pay them 900$ for the service. In effect, the credit settlement company manages to gain profit. This is also a good option if nothing else is available. One thing you have to remember is that the law prohibits credit settlement companies from asking advance payments. Hence, they should be able to settle the debt with your credit card company before asking for payments from you. This is a law passed pursuant to the Federal Trade Commission Rule in 2010.

Other (Unusual) Ways to Pay Off your Debt Quickly

Borrowing from your Life Insurance
Borrow against your life insurance to help you pay off unpaid debts that are causing your credit score to fall. This is possible when done against life insurance with cash value. In effect, you are borrowing from your own money. The only upside of this is that the interest rate will be marginally lower than your credit card debt.

How will this work for your credit score? Borrowing against your insurance simply gives you the chance to wipe off the debt from your credit history and therefore improve your credit utilization ratio. Instead of paying the credit card company, you will be making payments to your insurer at a lower interest rate. The beauty here is that loans from your insurance company is not counted when computing credit scores. After all, you are borrowing the same money that you paid to the insurance company.

Note however that this loan must be paid as soon as possible. If not, there is a good chance that your insurer will not provide coverage in the event that you die before repayment. Failure to do so will increase the burden on your loved ones and will significantly decrease the redeemed amount from the insurer.

Balance Transfer Offers
Some banks offer promotions to entice potential clients into signing up in their bank. These balance transfer offers essentially allows you to transfer unpaid amounts to the bank and pay only a smaller interest rate within a specific period. How this works is that the bank will pay off any outstanding debts you may have from the credit card company and take the place as your new lender. The bank will then impose a smaller interest rate but only for a specific period of time. Afterwards, the bank may increase the interest rate depending on previously agreed upon considerations.

What's important to keep in mind when using balance transfer offers is that you only have a small window of opportunity to pay off the debt. Within the period you are allowed to pay a small interest rate, you should do everything you can to pay off the full debt. Otherwise, you might find yourself struggling through a heavier burden financially. Balance transfer offers are only best used when you have sufficient money to pay the full debt plus interest rate at a time when the interest rate is still at its lowest. This means you should do the math quickly and predict overall payment. Also consider how much the interest rate would be AFTER the promo period. If it is equal to or less than the old credit card, then you won't have a problem using this new card for future transactions.

There are also balance transfer credit cards that work under the same principle. With this setup you have the option of transferring your credit to a different lender or perhaps even the same lender upon renegotiation. In the same vein, balance transfer credit cards only have a small interest rate during the promo period. Afterwards, the interest rate may increase which means that payments must be made quickly.

Borrowing from Family and Friends

As unappealing as it may sound, borrowing from friends and family might be your best choice in order to payoff lingering debt. This option helps you avoid interest rates or at least allow you to enjoy smaller interest rates in view of friends and family relations. Of course, you would want to make sure that the debt is fully paid as promised, otherwise this might cause a rift on your relationship with this person.

Borrowing from Your 401(k)

Most 401(k) allows you to borrow as much as fifty percent of the value of your account or fifty thousand dollars whichever is smaller. If you think that borrowing from your 401(k) will help wipe out most of your debt, then it would be a good idea to simply opt for this repayment plan. Like with borrowing from your insurance, borrowing from your 401(k) will allow you to enjoy lower interest rates. Note however, that your 401 (k) is a long-term investment specially built for retirement. Therefore, you want to make sure that it is properly paid as soon as possible.

Chapter 16: Step 9 – Speeding Up the Payment Process

OK – so in the last Chapter, we talked about how you can negotiate the situation in order to make your debt payments more manageable. The goal in the last Chapter is to simply reduce the overall burden so you don't have to reduce your expenses on necessities like food and utilities.

Once the main debt has been reduced, it's time to develop payment methods that speed up the payment process of your debts. The goal here is to pay recurring expenses while still managing to save a little for the delinquent debts. Understand – you WILL have a hard time here if the debts pile up. There is no way around it, so you'll have to budget around the debt and reduce frivolous spending.

Here are the typical debt payment methods that can speed up the process:

Different Debt Payment Methods

Debt avalanche

Debt avalanche is a straight-forward system utilized by borrowers with multiple credit cards and various interest rates. It works by making minimum payments on other credit cards and then using any remaining amount as additional payment for the credit card with the highest interest rate. This is a simple mathematical approach that allows you to wipe out the debt that will most likely cost you in the long run. Once debt with the highest interest rate has been paid, you can now proceed to the next loan with high interest rate.

Debt snowball
The debt avalanche is anchored on the principle of quick payments. In contrast, the debt snowball takes into consideration the wavering motivation of the borrower when confronted with multiple debts. The primary principle of this technique is to pay off the smallest debts first regardless of the interest rate attached with the debt.

The goal is to see quick progress and have looming debts wiped out quickly to improve your motivation. Once you notice that the number of bills are decreasing, this gives you a sense of satisfaction which lets you save more and focus on wiping out the other debts.

Apps for Debt Management
The main reason why people have a hard time keeping track and paying of their debts is because they find it tiresome and time consuming. Another issue is when it comes to small purchases that add up to hundreds of dollars at the end of the month. For example, your regular cup of coffee from Starbucks would cost 3USD every day. On a daily context, this might not seem much but multiply it over a period of 30 days and this will add up to 90USD per month. If you prefer the more complicated cups of coffee, then this can easily hit the 100USD mark.

So how do you fix this problem? How do you keep track of your expenses so that there will be more money remaining for debt payment?

The good news is there are currently several apps you can download on your phone to keep you up to date on your expenditures. These apps are made for easy use and lets you make quick entries throughout the day. Following are some of the best apps in the market today, some of which are even made for specific types of debt like Student Loans.

Quicken
Quicken is a comprehensive finance software that helps you create a complete budget plan on a monthly basis. The beauty of this software is that it has a specific function which lets you plan your budget around a fixed debt. Most users utilize this software to speed up debt management and payment.

Quicken also has the function of automatically generating minimum payment plus interest for your credit cards and other monthly billing. This way, you can, at a glance, easily see how these monthly expenses can affect your savings, debt payment, and living expenditures. The app even lets you access your credit score so you can have real time information on the changes to your score. This is an excellent way to keep you motivated until all the looming debt has been paid off. Quicken is a paid application which costs around 29.99$ for a year. It is primarily used for Windows and Mac operating systems.

Undebt.IT

Of course, if you are here trying to reduce your debt and improve your credit score, then chances are you don't have the extra finances to pay for a debt management software. Undebt.IT is a free software that gives you preset repayment plans for existing loans. It actually uses several repayment plans such as debts snowball and debt avalanche which we already discussed.

The app recognizes the fact that different plans work for different people. This is why the app lets you switch from one plan to another depending on what works for you.

Almost all apps come with some sort of motivational information to keep you on track. In the case of Undebt.IT, the app provides a projected graph showing how much you would be able to pay off if you stick to the preset plan given by the software. It also provides projection of the total amount of interest you'll pay for the debt. The app is completely free, but you can upgrade to a premium version for a one-time payment of 12USD.

Mint

Mint has been in the market for years now, considered as the gold standard for budgeting apps. The account synchronizes with your personal profile so that any spending you might do on your cards would be automatically updated through the app.

It works in tandem with several banks and credit card companies to pull information from your personal account. Now, this might seem alarming considering how this puts your security at risk. After all, you don't want a third-party application gaining access to your financial information like your credit card and bank account numbers. So far however, there have been no negative reports or information leaks connected with the use of Mint. In fact, you have the option of "forgetting" certain accounts so that they are removed from app storage. Just remember that whenever you access financial applications, always use your personal internet line. Avoid opening these apps when using public wireless internet.

Another cool feature of this app is its customization. You can create folders allocating your finances to specific expenses such as groceries or insurance payments. Those with investments like IRA can also link their accounts to Mint for a quick overview of the market.

ChangEd
Available for both iPhone and Android users, this debt payment app will cost you just 1USD every month. Recognizing the huge student loan debts held by many millennials today, the ChangEd app makes it easier for students to pay off existing student loans. According to studies, the average student debt as of 2017 was 26900USD. With the help of this app, the payment life could be reduced to 3-5 years depending on your financial capacity.

The app works by analyzing your spending habits and then syncing with your bank account. It then provides you with an overview of your expenditures to help you better plan your future spending.

One unique thing about this app is that it uses an accounting principle of round offs. In accounting, the general rule is to round up purchases to make sure that you have sufficient budget for particular expenses. For example, if there is an estimated expenditure of 1381, an accounting entry would be rounded up to 1400. This is exactly what ChangEd does with your expenses. It then simply sets aside the remaining amount into a separate account. In the given example, there would be a "change" of around 19USD. This is a fairly small amount that you might not even notice. However, ChangEd will make sure that these small amounts will accumulate over time. Once the accumulated amount reaches at least 100USD, it will be automatically used to pay off your student loan which forms part of the credit score.

Credit Card Payoff
The bad news about this particular debt payment app is that it is only available for Android users. The good news is that it is completely for free.

The app is focused on creating time-based goals for the payment of debt. It offers comparisons of different debts and their corresponding interest rates. Automatically the app will tell you which debts have the highest interest rates when paid over the life of the loan. This will tell you which debts should be paid off first so that you won't expend additional cash on interest alone. Simply put – it uses the debt avalanche approach.

What's cool about this app is that it lets you experiment. For example, how much faster would you be able to pay off the loan if you increase your payments by 50 or 75USD per month? This lets you set a motivational goal to speed up payments and completely wipe off the debt within the period allotted. Finally, all the information provided in the app comes via easy to read charts.

Chapter 17: Step 10 – Your New and Better Credit Targets

Let's do a quick recap. After discussing how to better manage debt, we talked about how to pay off the debts you have right now in a quick manner. In this Chapter, our goal is to rebuild the debt or simply put – teach you how to deal with current debts as opposed to the delinquent ones.

So once you've eliminated all the negatives or started to eliminate them from your history, the next step is to rebuild your credit. This means arranging all your future transactions to reflect a better credit score. The goal is to raise it enough for you to have an acceptable credit rating and gain immediate acceptance should you choose to apply for a loan.

But what exactly is a good credit score? From here on out, understand that when we say "credit score", we're talking about FICO standards.

In a previous Chapter, we talked about the typical classifications for credit score with 670 to 739 the "official" numbers for

Good. Understand however that for purposes of getting your loan applications accepted, a score of 670 or above is not absolutely necessary. After all, lenders have their personal standards on what is acceptable. The score is only a "clue" for them, but the decision is still on the lender to accept or reject a proposal.

Good credit score therefore really depends on what you are trying to apply for. Generally, anything beyond 580 is considered good and will allow you to gain access to some of the best credit lines in the country. Understand however that credit card companies have their own private criteria. While some may have no problem accepting a credit score of 580 or below, others will stick to an absolute minimum when allowing applications.

Your Credit Card Goals for a Better Score

If you want to control or improve your credit score, the best place to start would be your credit card. According to studies, the typical American holds an average of 4 credit cards with an average debt of around 1154USD per card. Compared to large loans, credit card debts are easier to navigate through and even small changes can do so much to your credit report.

What kind of credit card is best to help with credit scores?
Secured credit cards are the best because they are made especially for people with bad credit scores. An extensive discussion is available in Chapter 14.

How much debt to credit ratio should you maintain?
As already mentioned, the golden percentage for debt to credit ratio is 30 percent. For mortgage loans, a debt to credit ratio of 45 percent is sufficient while it is always possible to improve these rates, these are the targets you want to reach before applying for any type of loan.

How many cards should you own?
The number of credit cards that you own should not be more than 3 at any given time. Obviously, this would change depending on your financial capacity. Since you are reading this book, there is an assumption that you are overwhelmed by the amount of your debt. That being the case, the best course of action is to

simply keep the credit cards you have right now and do not open another one until you are confident with your financial situation.

Again, this goes back to the principle of debt and credit ratio. As much as possible, you do not want to reduce the amount you can utilize by closing a credit card. On the other hand, opening a brand-new credit card may lead to higher debt in the future because of an increased interest rate from the new credit card.

How to make payments for a better credit score?
Let's say you are still using that credit card and therefore want to keep it open. Proper management of this particular account would contribute towards a better credit score for you. This simply means paying your debt on the card, making sure you never make late payments or below minimum ones. You should also keep in mind that credit utilization ration rule which requires that your credit should only be 30 percent of the allowed debt. Hence, if you currently have a maximum credit limit of 1000USD, your debt on that should always be 300USD or below.

Your Credit Score Goal for Better Mortgage Loans

A mortgage is perhaps the biggest single loan you would have in your lifetime. This is something you would commit to for the next 30 or 40 years of your life so you would want to make sure that you are getting the best possible interest rate.

For the purpose of getting mortgage on a house however, you want to have a credit score of at least 600 with a debt to credit ratio of 45 percent. With this set up, you should be able to get a "fair" interest rate. For the best interest rates however, you would want to get a score of 700 and above while this is possible, it's not an easy job to do and might only delay your desire to gain mortgage loan. Hence, once you hit 600, you can apply for larger loans and hopefully get an interest rate that you can afford.

Keep in mind however, that if you are married your good credit score will be weighed together with the credit score of your spouse. Hence, if you have 600 and your spouse has 400, you may still get a bad interest rate.

Utilize Score Boosting Programs

Credit Bureaus like Experian and FICO often provide programs that give your credit score an additional boost. For example, Experian boost can thicken your credit profile by adding your utility bills and telecommunication bills to your credit history. Ordinarily, these are transactions that are not included in your credit report. For most people however, these are the same transactions that are almost always paid on time. By adding this to your credit report, you gain the advantage of having on time payments through other accounts.

Currently, there are two free programs that can help boost your credit report. First is Experian Boost and UltraFICO. There are also paid programs available which include, eCredable Lift, PayYourRent, and RentTrack.

Self-Reporting your Credit Information

Self-reporting your credit information directly to the Credit Bureau is not possible. The fact is Credit Bureaus, in order to maintain the integrity of their information, must accept data only from accredited furnishers. The good news is that there are third parties who can help you report your personal information and give your credit history an additional advantage when applying for a loan. This companies work by expanding the coverage of your credit report to include items that are ordinarily excluded from the history. This includes rents and internet bills.

The downside of this technique is that you'll have to pay these third-party companies in order to report positive credit information. There is also the possibility that the furnished information is already included in your credit report. This often happens when a property management company handles your rental transactions.

So let's set the stage right now.

Your credit score goal should be 670. Wherever you might be in life right now, that's the goal we're trying to reach here.

Chapter 18: Business Credit Score for Business Owners

If you own a business, this Chapter is for you. If not however, you might want to skip this Chapter and proceed to the next one.

One thing you have to understand is that a personal credit score and the credit score of your business are two separate entities. One does not affect the other – unless of course, you are using your personal credit card to make purchases for your business.

Simply put, if you are a business owner – you want to maintain a separate business credit card for the business and name the account for your business account. This way, your business credit score will not affect your personal credit score.

Computing a Business Score

There is a distinct difference between a personal credit score (PCS) and a business credit score (BCS). For one thing, they actually don't have the same range. A PCS comes with a 300 to 850 range. A BCS on the other hand only comes with a 0 to 100 range.

Access to your Business Credit Score

When it comes to your PCS, only a select number of individuals can have access to the information. In the case of your employers, they can't even access it without a written assent on your part. What if you order your own business score? Well, this is where another big distinction should be noted. With a business credit score, you ALWAYS have to pay – even if it's your own business.

This is not the same for a business credit score. A BCS is public and anyone who wants to access the information can do it upon payment. This is really for the protection of anyone who deals with you – especially if you make purchases on credit for the business.

Credit Bureaus for Business Credit Scores

Now, the credit bureaus for businesses are a tad different than personal ones. There is Equifax and Experian – but TransUnion is not on the list. Instead, you have to direct your inquiries to

Contents of the Report

If you are going to order your Business Credit Score, keep in mind that payment will always be asked for. The extent of the information included in the report may vary, depending on where you'll be requesting the data. Here's what you need to know:

Dun and Bradstreet
Price: 61.99USD
Click here to order.
Inclusions:
- Gives you 6 months of access to report
- Provides you with their calculated recommendation for a credit limit
- Commercial credit score – this tells you the chances of a delinquent payment being made on the bills for the following 12 months. It ranges from 101 to 670 with a low score showing a higher chance of missing or failing to make payments.
- Financial stress score – this is a unique scoring system for business owners. It predicts the possibility of the business actually failing within the next 12 months. The scoring is anywhere from

1001 to 1610 with the lower score creating a higher chance of failure.
- Credit summary
- Paydex score
- Industry payment benchmarks

Equifax
Price: 99.95USD
Click here to order.
Inclusions:
- Business credit risk score – this calculates the chances of severe delinquency of the business. The score can be anywhere from 101 to 992, taking into consideration the size of the company, the credit limit, revolving accounts, and various more.
- Business failure score – as the name suggests, this takes into consideration the chances of the business failing within the next 12 months. The score ranges from 1000 to 1610.
- Credit summary
- Credit risk score
- Public records
- Payment index – this measures the timeliness of payments made by the business at a scale of 0 to

100. Unlike the Paydex Score however, this scoring does not intend to predict how a company would pay in the future. It simply provides a history of how the business fared in the past. How lenders will interpret this information is completely up to them.

- Business failure score -
- Payment trend and comparison to industry norm

Experian
Price: 39.35USD
Click here to order.
Inclusions:

- Credit summary
- Public records
- Payment summary trends
- Business credit score – this scoring type ranges from 0 to 100 and are derived from information more than just your payment history. Hence, it's actually a lot different from the previous two credit reports. Other information that are taken into account include suppliers, legal filings, company background, public

records, and even records from collection agencies.

Tips for Improving Business Credit Score

Improving your business credit score more or less follows the same principles as improving your personal credit score.

Using the right business account
Since businesses affect the public, the government imposes certain standards or regulations that need to be followed. For example, businesses have a federal tax identification number or an employer identification number. This is the primary tracking device used by the credit bureaus to find out how much debt a business has. Simply put all the debts you had listed under your federal tax identification number is taken to consideration while computing your business score.

The problem here is that not all businesses operate using business accounts. Sole proprietors will often use their personal accounts to make loans and payments in favor of their business. While this may make it appear that your business has o debt, it also removes the possibility of the business building a good credit history. The simple answer to this is to open business accounts and vendor accounts. In the long run, this would also help your personal finances because the business debts will be attributed to the juridical entity and not to you personally.

Opening a credit line
Many business owners prefer to pay cash for their operational expenses. While this might seem like a sound business decision, paying cash outright will not help you build a good credit history. In fact, there will be no credit history to speak off. Should you need a loan in the future, it could be difficult for you to gain approval because the lenders will have no information on which to base their decision.

Reporting payments
Loans made by one business to another should also form part of your business credit score. For example, let's say that you own a restaurant with an open account from several suppliers. Even if you make timely payments to the supplier, these payments will not be recorded into your business credit

history unless the supplier reports it to the bureau. For this reason, if you want to build a good business credit score, it's important to find vendors who submit their account information to regulating bodies.

If your supplier does not do this, you have an option of switching into another supplier or simply ask this one to start reporting information.

Disputing information on your business credit score
Disputes made under your business account are done in the same way as personal accounts. The only difference would be the address of the bureau where the dispute will be sent.

Declaring Bankruptcy in Business
Much like with personal debts, businesses can declare bankruptcy under chapter 11 of the United States bankruptcy law. Chapter 11 is built specifically for businesses as opposed to Chapter 7 and Chapter 13.

Chapter 11 is akin to Chapter 13 which provides for re organization of debt. Instead of completely wiping out the unpaid balance, Chapter 11 allows the arrangement of debt so that the company would be able to make routine payments within the scope of their monthly income. Note that this is an option resorted to by large companies like Enron. This is often an expensive and long process but will not have a huge impact on the credit score of the business. This is because while Chapter 11 bankruptcy extends the payment period, it would still require the business to pay off its debt completely.

Chapter 19: Myths and Fallacies About Credit Scores

So far, we've done our best to talk about the facts surrounding credit scores and what you can do to help improve your standing. Unfortunately, there are still misconceptions out there and, in this Chapter, we'll try to address these issues.

Your Credit Score is NOT Universal
It bears repeating that your credit score from TransUnion is not the same with your score from Experian and so on. While they may all use the same basic formula or a variation thereof, the fact is that the data used by each one may vary. Hence, be prepared for a bit of difference between the bureaus – with a few points of difference still acceptable among the three. It's up to you to decide whether the difference in points is an acceptable one. For most, as long as the difference in points keeps them within the same classification (Excellent, Good, Very Good) then they're happy with the results.

Income Does NOT Determine your Credit Score

Your credit score will not increase because your income did. It's never a factor when the bureaus compute your score. In fact, it's doubtful that they even know what income bracket you fall in. The main reason why people with a high income have a good credit score has to do with their ability to pay off their debts. After all, if you are pulling in thousands every month, then you are also capable of paying off existing debts. Note though that even a millionaire can have a terrible credit score if they're borrowing extensively.

Credit Blacklists do NOT Exist
There is no such thing as a credit blacklist. Credit bureaus do not keep a list of people that they automatically deem as bad debtors. The persons who determine whether you should be awarded credit are the lenders, banks, or landlords using the score provided by the bureau. Hence, even if you have a Good credit score rating, some banks may still reject your loan if they require a Very Good rating before extending loans.

Parking Tickets and Library Fines are NOT Included in Your Credit Report

There are small debts or expenses that you are obligated to pay off – but they're not considered as part of your credit report. You probably saw that they're not in the list as written in a previous Chapter. Even if they're sent to a collection agency – they still don't form part of your credit report.

Late Payments are NOT Removed After You Paid off the Debt

Understand that credit scores are based off your credit HISTORY and not your current credit status. While your debt to credit ratio is taken into consideration, all the transactions that led you up to that point matters more. Hence, even if you managed to pay off a debt, the fact that you made late payments on it will still be taken into consideration. The whole transaction will NOT be wiped out simply because all the debts have been paid.

Not Having any Credit is NOT a Good Thing

Most people are proud of the fact that they do not have any debts or that they do not own any credit card. While this is admirable, this does not bode well for your credit score. Remember, the credit score is computed based on your past behavior with debts. Not having any debts, therefore, means that you have ZERO credit score. This can be a problem because in the event that you apply for a loan, the lender would not have any information on which to base their decision. Having a credit card, therefore, is often a good idea simply for the purpose of establishing and building your credit.

Disputed Bills are Part of Your Credit History

There is this belief that a disputed bill will not be recorded by the credit bureau. For example, you believe that you only have an unpaid amount of 1000USD. However, the lender is claiming 1500USD. Let's say that you want to dispute this amount with the lending company by sending a letter and holding the payment in abeyance until you agree on the proper amount. You might think that the credit card company will also hold off reporting the credit, but this is not the case. A late payment will always be a late payment whether or not it is being disputed.

So how do you solve this problem? The best way is to launch a dispute even before the bill becomes past due. If this is not possible, you have the option of paying the amount required by the lender and simply demanding a refund. You can also ask the credit bureau to attach a note with each credit report saying that the unpaid amount is under dispute and therefore unpaid until the dispute has been settled.

Debit Cards Do NOT Help with Credit Scores

Debit cards are merely extensions of the money you have in the bank. Whenever you use a debit card, you are simply authorizing the bank to send money from your own account in favor of someone else. Therefore, there is no loan occurring in this transaction. Using a debit card is as good as using cash when making payments so it won't be part of your credit history. If you are using this method, you might as well get a secured credit card to build a history.

It Takes a Long Time for a Good Credit Score to Turn Bad

Unfortunately, it can take as little as 6 months for your good credit score to plummet. All it takes are as series of unpaid debts or late payments for the average to go down. Even worse, upon problems, someone with a high starting score can experience a bigger drop as opposed to someone who has a low starting score. Hence, do not be complacent. If you have a good score, put habits in place to guarantee that it stays that way.

One thing you should note is that good credit takes time to build. Some people would tell you it takes 6 months – but that's not true at all. Six months refers to how long it takes for you to *establish credit*. What does this mean? Well, imagine that you just turned 21 and finally got your very own credit card. It will take 6 months of owning this card before credit bureaus will collect your information and start to build your credit report.

Turning a negative into a positive takes a longer time. Remember – bad financial transactions will stay on your report for 7 to 10 years, depending on the situation. Hence, if you defaulted on a particular debt or had consistently late payments, only time can make it go away. Turning negative into a positive therefore means you have to overwhelm your bad credit history with positive actions.

But again – how long does it take? Well, if you want an actual number – then that will take 7 years of consistently good financial decisions.

Checking your Credit will NOT Hurt your Credit Score

Remember what we said about soft and hard pulls. Ordering your credit score or even inquiring into your credit history will be considered as a soft pull. Therefore, there will no impact on your credit report. In fact, it may be seen as a measure of responsibility in a person.

Using Only One Card Will NOT Help your Credit Score

There are instances where people with only one credit card and consistently paid bills still have a bad credit score. This usually happens when the single credit card is used over and over again. Despite the fact that minimum payments are made every month, the credit utilization remains negative. This is because there is no dispersion of the borrowed amount across several cards.

In this instance it is often better to open brand new accounts.

Hence, opening a new credit card can actually help your credit score in specific situations, as discussed in a previous Chapter. Of course, this will only work if you have a credit that will not require a high interest rate on the part of the lender. Opening a new account will impact your debt to credit ratio, allowing the ceiling to increase, provided that you do not borrow any amount on this brand-new account.

Chapter 20: Long Term Planning – Sustaining a Good Credit Score

So far, we've been talking about how you can fix past transactions or mistakes you've made that led to your bad credit score. We also set the stage and made a commitment towards a credit score of 670. In this chapter we will talk about how you will handle future transactions so that you can take that first step towards this new goal.

The truth is everyone knows how to maintain a good credit score. The principles are simple: borrow only what you can pay off and always pay your debts on time. The problem here is while it is easy on theory, the practice is much more difficult. It's a lot like trying to lose weight. Everyone knows that in order to lose weight, you have to eat less and exercise more, but doing it is very difficult. The same goes with maintaining a good credit score. The key therefore is to cultivate habits that promote proper financial control. This is exactly what we are going to discuss in this particular chapter.

Maintaining Good Records of All your Financial Transactions

If you noticed, a large part of repairing your credit involves sending the credit bureau with information about your transactions. You need to be able to prove to the bureau that the transactions reported to their organization are incorrect and that your information is the right one. This is why it's crucial that you maintain a record of all your transactions including the date, the amount, and the person or entity involved. Now, this can be tiresome and may take up much of your time. However, you will find that this will serve you in the long run and give you an additional security in the process.

There are currently tons of ways for you to make this process easier. For example, some people create email accounts simply for the purpose of storing all their information. You can take pictures of your receipts or reports and upload them to your email for easy storage. Some people use Facebook messengers and send snapshots or screenshots to themselves. This will make it easier for you to retrieve them as well as remember

what date or what time they were
received.

Keeping up with your Debt to Credit Ratio

Your debt to credit ratio should be less
than 50 percent at all times. As
previously mentioned in this book, 30
percent is the ideal amount, but this
might not be always possible. At the very
least, make a commitment towards 50
percent and never allow yourself to go
beyond that.

Computing debt to credit ratio is not that
difficult. It is often displayed as
percentages to illustrate, you have an
existing debt of 1000$ and have a credit
limit of 5000USD, your credit ratio
would be 1000 divided by 500 for a total
of 20 percent. Using this formula, you
can always check your debt to credit ratio
and adjust accordingly depending on the
situation.

Investing on Insurance

One of the primary reasons why people
have a hard time maintaining their credit
is due to emergency needs. In most cases,
an accident will happen that requires a
person to dip into their savings.

Unfortunately, if there are no savings, the individual may use their credit card or utilize lenders to make payments. This is a problem that can be easily solved by setting up insurance through reputable insurance companies. This provides additional security on your person and should prevent you from resorting to lenders. The beauty here is that insurance companies do not rely on credit score when computing premiums. As previously discussed, borrowing on your insurance is also an option should you need to settle debts.

Staying up to Date with your Credit Report

There are people today in their 30's who have never ordered their credit report. They are therefore shocked when after ordering their report for the first time, find that they score is below ideal. I hope that because you are reading this book, you have already realized the error of ignoring your credit history.

From here on out therefore, you should order your credit report from all three credit bureaus every year. We already talked about how to order these reports and the fact that they are available for free once every year. Therefore, you can actually have your report delivered to you once every 4 months. Consistently ordering your report will give you the chance to countercheck the information included in there as well as notice any red flags indicative of identity theft.

Consistent, Timely, and Minimum Payments

This is a pretty popular technique but bears repeating: always pay your debts on time even if it is at a minimum. Late payments are better than no payment at all. If you have several credit cards, it's often a good idea to zero out the one with the highest interest rate and just leave it open. This will help lower your credit utilization ratio.

A common technique is to make maximum payments to the card with the highest interest rate until it is completely paid off. For example, you have 3 cards with interest rates of 3, 5, and 10 percent. You can pay only the minimum for the credit cards with the lower interest rate and pay as much as possible with the 10 percent credit card. This will severely lower your expenses once the credit card at 10 percent has been completely paid off. From there, you can focus on the second highest credit card and so on. Note though, that for purposes of credit score, these cards should be left open.

Zero Based Budgeting

This technique encourages you to make every dollar work. Simply put, every amount is accounted for in your budget, down to the last centavo. Even before getting your paycheck, you already know where and how the money will be spent. This requires a full attention to detail and leaves no wiggle room, which can be frustrating and fulfilling all at the same time. Now, this might seem like a lot of work but there are actually budgeting applications designed using this particular budgeting technique. The popular YNAB app is a good choice for download if you think this plan would work for you.

Who could best benefit from this? If you are an impulse shopper – you'll find that Zero Based Budgeting is the perfect choice for you.

Envelope system

Envelope system is a technique that physically allows you to allocate your cash depending on what is needed for the next month. To illustrate you can have several envelopes with the words "grocery," "bills," and "pets," written on top of each one. The envelope system tells you to put inside the budget you have for each particular account. You will then use only the money placed in that particular envelope for the expenses related to it.

The beauty of this technique is that it forces you to rely on cash alone when creating a budget. This actually has a psychological effect in that cash transactions makes you more aware of how much you are spending and therefore lets you exercise control over yourself. This is in contrast with buying solely on credit cards which leaves you remove from the situation.

But won't this mess up your credit history? Not really. When used in conjunction with automatic payments, the Envelope System works beautifully. Hence, fixed debts like mortgage loans or auto loans are automatically paid from your account. You can then withdraw everything you need for the month/week and allocate them in envelopes and make payments directly with cash.

Who could best benefit from this? If you are the kind of person who just loves to use their credit card for buying, this will be perfect and will leave you more aware of what you are buying.

The 50/30/20 Budget
This is perhaps one of the simplest budgeting techniques commended by people. The approach is simple: you categorize your expenses into three. First are needs, second are wants, and third are savings. Simply put, 50 percent of your take home money should be used to pay for your needs. This include foods and groceries. The 30 percent should go to the things that you want and finally 20 percent should go to your savings.

The beauty of this budgeting technique is that you immediately know how much you take away for savings. This 50/30/20 rule should be applied in conjunction with "savings first" principle. Hence, once you get your monthly pay, compute the 20 percent first and set it aside on a separate account. The remaining 80 percent should be used in budgeting while making sure that the 20 percent in your savings account remains untouched.

The primary downfall of this technique is that it can be difficult to distinguish between what you need and what you want. For example, when it comes to food the lines can be blurry. To illustrate, do you want the milk tea, or do you need the milk tea? The classifications can be quite confusing and may lead you to buy things you want instead of the things that you actually need. A good approach is to start with the things you absolutely cannot live without and then start from there. Some people remove one item at a time from their grocery list and see how they fare without it. It's a trial and error approach so try to be patient.

The 80/20 Budget

This technique is even simpler than the 50/30/20 budget. Under this method, you set aside the 20 percent as savings and then use the remaining amount for your day to day expenses. This requires a measure of control on your part to make sure that you don't spend the full amount until the next paycheck comes in.

Scheduling your Payments to Guarantee on Time Payments

There are situations where people who have sufficient income still have bad credit scores. This can occur because despite the fact that they have the cash to make plenty payments, they always forget to make such payments on time. Keep in mind that late payments are heavily factored into credit scores. Therefore, as part of your effort to improve your credit score, there should be a system in place to make sure that all bills are paid on time.

Fortunately, there are dozens of ways that this can be done. Even a simple pen and paper approach can help remind you of due dates for credit card debts and utilities. Mobile phones today also come with notification settings that you can use as a reminder for payment of revolving debts. Third party applications which can be customized to your personal preferences also exists to help with budgeting and timely payments.

Some banks today even offer automatic payment of debts every month without the need for any action on your part. This is a good idea for fixed expenses such as your mortgage loan, personal loans, or even to pay your Netflix membership.

Adding to the Income

It's pretty basic – if your current income is not enough to cover all your expenses, you can either reduce the expenses or increase the income. Now, this basic formula sounds simple on theory but when practiced, it requires a whole new discussion and a whole new book. It bears stressing however that this is always an option if you believe that you are capable of physically, emotionally, and psychologically handling added responsibilities to increase your income.

Utilize Budgeting Apps

We previously talked about apps to pay for debts – but what about apps that help you manage day to day expenses? There are software today that can do this beautifully so that you can keep track of even the smallest expenses and then do a quick monthly recap so you would be aware of how much you actually spend on a particular item. Remember the coffee story we had a few Chapters ago? There are apps today that will help you log in those daily coffee purchases and give you the total amount at the end of the month.

YNAB

For a heavily committed budget, YNAB is your go-to application. As mentioned, it uses zero-based budgeting but in a much more efficient manner because the app does all the logging in and remembering for you. With this app, you can connect your bank accounts, create goals, add to savings, customize your spending, and so on. If YNAB would be a weight loss technique, it would be calorie-counting because of the highly targeted approach. It's not free though – it costs 89USD a year or 11.99 a month. A 34-day free trial is available.

EveryDollar

This budgeting app lets you track what you spend and what you plan to spend your money on. Again, it's a zero-based budgeting technique but at a more affordable version of ZERO dollars. With the basic free version, you should be able to get most of the useful features for daily use. If you want to upgrade however, this will cost you around 129.99USD every year. Syncing your bank account to your expenses is a feature only available on the Premium level.

Personal Capital

This app is primarily used for investment management. It works with the help of robo-advisors and human financial advisors to help with your finances. While it has features for budgeting, the primarily purpose of this is to trace your credit card accounts, 401k, IRAs, loans, and mortgages. Hence, it handles the BIG ONES instead of the smaller expenses you make on a day to day basis. Along with these features, you can also customize categories, create snapshots of your spending, and even keep track of your net worth.

GoodBudget

This particular app utilizes the envelope system as discussed. The beauty of this however is that it lets you share the information with other people – like Google Docs. In a family setting therefore, you and your partner can both access the app and find out how the other person is adjusting the expenses to meet demands. This makes it easier for the two of you to agree on certain expenses and let everyone know exactly how the money is being used. One downside of this however is that you can't sync it with your bank account – which makes perfect sense since the whole system relies on a cash-basis budget. There is a free version with a limited number of envelopes and only shareable between two people. A Plus version costs 6USD per month and can be accessed by up to 5 devices and unlimited envelope options.

Mvelopes
Another app that uses envelope style budgeting is Mvelopes which offers basic access to a cash-type spending habit. It's fairly easy to use and lets you enjoy real-time budget matching which is perfect if you have a sudden urge to purchase something. The app tells you if, after doing all the computations, you have money to spare for coffee or for a good massage. You can also connect it with several financial accounts with the setup open for reset if needed.

Google Docs and Google Excel
While not an app, this is definitely a good way to share or log in your financial information through the internet. It offers security, the ease of share ability, and editing, without any expenditure on your part. Of course, there is the issue of creating an excel system completely from scratch – but once you manage to do this,

everything else can be quickly and easily done.

Obviously, these are just some of the apps available online that can help you with budgeting. There are literally thousands out there today that will fit you, regardless of whether you need one for Android, iPhone, laptop, or even a cross-platform software. It's a hit and miss situation and as you develop better spending habits, you will be able to find the perfect app that meets you needs.

Getting Emotional and Psychological Help

Financial stress is not something you should shrug off and oftentimes, it's not something you can go through alone. The fact is that according to studies, people who are trying to achieve a goal are more likely to reach that goal if they make themselves accountable to someone. For example, if you are trying to lose weight, then it helps to have someone who guides you through the process and make you accountable for what you eat or when you work out. The same is true for money problems.

Today, there are groups, organizations, or perhaps personal friends, who can help you through the process.

Financial Counseling
In the United States, you can seek help via the National Debt Helpline where you can talk to financial counsellors, often for free. They can provide added insight and connect you to a community that can offer support during this stressful time. Small business owners can also call 1800-413-828 if they're struggling with finances because of COVID19, bushfires, or any other calamity that might be occurring in their area. There are also counselors specifically for rural farmers affected by natural calamities.

Financial Therapist
You can also seek help from a financial therapist designed not only to guide you through your finances but also to help you create sound financial habits and decision-making skills. The Association for Financial Counseling and Planning Education (AFCPE) is the primary source for good therapists who can help you during this time. The group maintains high standards to make sure therapists offer good quality service. Of course,

these financial therapists aren't free, but given that they specialize on this particular issue, they are more likely to offer their services at an affordable and reasonable rate.

Online Groups and Communities
You might be surprised at the amount of Facebook groups, online forums, and communities that are designed to help people go through debt and money problems. There are tons of communities today with in-depth information about finances, credit scores, and debt management – all given with zero payment necessary on your part. There is something to be said about the strength of groups and with the internet, you can do all of this while remaining anonymous, therefore giving you the chance to really vent out and be honest with the information.

Friends and Family
Finally, there is always the close people around you to help with the emotional toll that the financial problems may cause. Do not be afraid to seek advice from the people you truly trust.

UNDERSTAND – you can seek the help of someone no matter what stage you are in this book. Even if you are just starting to order your credit report or if you are already trying to negotiate with the lenders – you always have the option to bring someone in to help you deal with the stress. There is not right or wrong time to find help.

Conclusion

To wrap it up – credit scores aren't permanent. They are the result of bad financial decisions, but they can also be resolved through good financial decisions. Do not let yourself be taken down by the depression and anxiety that comes with money problems. Through this book, I hope that you gained some perspective on how to handle your money AND create a good platform for future transactions.

The next step now is to follow the instructions in this book and get this party started! It might take a few months or even a year to gradually see the improvements in your credit score, but I promise that it will come. Constantly motivate yourself and one day, you will find yourself free of these financial burdens with a credit score that causes credit card companies to come knocking on your door with all kinds of offer.

We hope that you've taken the words of this book to heart and create a system that works for you. Understand that this is not a one-time thing. If you feel yourself wavering, read this book again and realign yourself. It's perfectly natural to lose a bit of your motivation but if you do, never think that you can't get back on track again. You can!

RESIST TEMPTATION! Stay on path. Good luck!